The ICSA Guide to

Charity Accounting

REVISED SORP 2000 EDITION

Adrian J. L. Randall FCA, BSC (ECON.)

Published by ICSA Publishing Ltd
16 Park Crescent
London
W1B 1AH

Typeset in Sabon & ITC Franklin Gothic by
Paul Barrett Book Production, Cambridge

Printed and bound in Great Britain by
TJ International Ltd., Padstow, Cornwall

British Library Cataloguing in Publication Data

A catalogue record for this book is available from the British Library.

ISBN 1-86072-138-9

Contents

Preface and Acknowledgements

In 1998 *SORP and the Regulations – A Comprehensive Guide* was published. It was based on a series of articles I had written following the publication of the Charities Statement of Recommended Practice (SORP), 'Accounting by Charities', in October 1995. *SORP and the Regulations – A Comprehensive Guide* was intended for finance staff, independent examiners, auditors and anyone who either produced or monitored the accounts produced by a wide range of charities. Since 1998 there have been quite a few changes in the accounting world, not least the publication in October 2000 of the revised SORP, 'Accounting and Reporting by Charities', and the updated regulations. *The ICSA Guide to Charity Accounting* has been written to take account of all the changes that have occurred. As with my previous book it is a reference book, for dipping into rather than reading from cover to cover – hence the practical guide approach, but of course it can be read from beginning to end!

The book opens with a detailed introduction to charity accounting by setting out what a charity is and how charity accounting has developed over the last fifteen or so years. Chapter 2 sets out the regulatory framework, that is to say the law relating to charity accounting, and gives a detailed background to the rules. Chapter 2 also introduces the Statement of Recommended Practice (SORP) for charities, and so sets the historical scene for the next chapter. Chapter 3 summarises the main changes to the 1995 Charities SORP and expands on the general principles of the revised SORP. Chapters 4–8 look in some detail at specific aspects of the SORP following the format of that document; that is to say, Chapter 4 deals with the Trustees' Annual Report, Chapter 5 with Statement of Financial Activities (SOFA), Chapter 6 with the balance sheet, while Chapter 7 covers, for the few charities that will need to produce one, the cash flow statement. Finally, the disclosure of accounting policies and notes to the accounts are dealt with in Chapter 8.

The SORP itself has a number of special sections. These are dealt with in Chapters 9–12. The topics covered relate to the presentation of summary financial information and statements (Chapter 9), the somewhat complicated issue of consolidation (Chapter 10), how the SORP has pulled together all the issues relating to charitable companies (Chapter 11) and finally accounting for smaller charities (Chapter 12) – an even more complicated area than it used to be. Chapter 13 moves away from the SORP and charity accounting to consider audit and independent examination.

Wherever appropriate examples have been used to illustrate the points being made. Many of these are taken from the Charity Commission's *SORP 2000: Example Reports and Accounts* because at the date of writing no charities had reported under the revised SORP. However, a number of examples are taken from actual charity accounts to illustrate those points in the SORP which have not been affected by the revisions.

The book concludes with a directory, which consists of a bibliography of further reading (books, Charity Commission leaflets and relevant journals) and a list of useful addresses and websites.

My thanks are due to all those who have assisted me in the production of this book, particularly Graham Smith of the Charity Commission for permission to use material originally produced by him; to members of the Charity Commission and the other members of the Charity Accounting Review Committee for permission to reproduce quotations from the SORP and SORP 2000: *Example Reports and Accounts*; and last but not least to my wife, Jenny, for all the assistance that she has given me in typing the original articles on which this book is based and the final version of it.

Extracts from various charities' reports and accounts to illustrate particular technical points are reproduced with kind permission of the charity including:

- Action Aid
- British Heart Foundation
- Cancer Research Campaign
- Changing Faces
- ChildLine
- Disabled Drivers' Association
- Engineering Construction Industry Training Board
- Mental Health Foundation
- The Royal Society
- Yorkshire Cancer Research Campaign

ADRIAN J. L. RANDALL
MAY 2001

1   Introduction to Charity Accounting

What is a charity?

Not all voluntary or not-for-profit organisations are charities. Tax legislation defines a charity as 'any body of persons or trust established for charitable purposes only', but does not define charitable purposes. To find out what are considered 'charitable purposes' one needs to go back to an Act of 1601 and a series of court decisions that have further developed and extended the definition.

The *Pemsel* decision (1891) sets out four general headings for charitable purposes, which are still accepted today. These are:

1   the relief of poverty;
2   the advancement of education;
3   the advancement of religion;
4   other purposes of a charitable nature beneficial to the community not falling under any of the other headings.

Where a charity's purposes fall within one of the first three headings, they are assumed to be charitable and for the benefit of the community, unless it is shown otherwise; but in the fourth category, a purpose must be shown to benefit the community in a way the law regards as charitable. A purpose contrary to public policy cannot be for the benefit of the community; not only will it not be charitable, but it will be void.

The Charity Commissioners for England and Wales (Charity Commission) will give a preliminary ruling on whether proposed purposes are charitable before an organisation is formed and a formal application for charitable status is made. However, it is worth noting at this stage that the Charity Commissioners have no jurisdiction in Scotland or Northern Ireland. The legislation in Scotland relevant to charities is the Law Reform (Miscellaneous Provisions) (Scotland) Act 1990 and in Northern Ireland charities are governed by the Charities Act (Northern Ireland) 1964 and the Charities (Northern Ireland) Order 1987. The charity authority in Scotland is the Inland Revenue and in Northern Ireland is the Department for Social Development.

A charity can be set up as a trust, an unincorporated association, a limited company, a friendly society, a housing association or by Act of Parliament. A trust is normally used where one or more individuals want to settle property that will be used permanently for charitable purposes. In simple terms, an unincorporated association is a club whose members aim to achieve a common charitable purpose. A charity normally will be incorporated as a company limited by guarantee without share capital.

The individuals in charge of running a charity are called trustees in the legislation governing charities, although they may go under other names in the charity's governing document. For example, a charity that is established as a company limited by guarantee has directors, who are therefore the trustees.

Trustees of a charity have the duty to ensure that the charity's income is used only for the charitable purposes of the charity and that the charity complies with all the legal requirements imposed on charities. The Charities Acts 1992 and 1993 made many changes to the law relating to charities. Their provisions cover charity accounts, charity documents, annual returns to the Charity Commissioners, public collections, the sale of land owned by charities and many other areas. The Charity Commission has produced a lucid guide to the law, *A Guide to the Charities Acts 1992 & 1993*, and charity trustees and administrators are recommended to read it.

Accounting developments leading to the Charities Acts 1992 and 1993

The following developments contributed to the Charities Acts 1992 and 1993:

- In 1984 the Accounting Standards Committee (ASC) issued a discussion paper on charity accounting.
- In 1985 the ASC issued an exposure draft (ED38) of a statement intended to provide some uniformity in charity accounts.
- In 1987 the Woodfield Report *Efficient Scrutiny of the Supervision of Charities* highlighted a number of deficiencies regarding the monitoring and control of charities by the Charity Commission.
- In February 1988 the Committee of Public Accounts issued a report, *Monitoring and Control of Charities in England and Wales*,

which was highly critical of the way in which charities were monitored and of charity financial management generally.

- In May 1988 the ASC issued Statement of Recommended Practice No. 2 (Accounting by Charities) (SORP 2).
- In the summer of 1988 the Charity Commission published *Charity Accounts – Consultation Paper*, seeking views of the sector at large.
- In September 1988 the Home Office issued a consultation paper *The Regulation of Charitable Appeals in England and Wales*.
- On 16 May 1989 the government presented its white paper *Charities: A Framework for the Future*, which included many of the recommendations of the Woodfield Report.
- At the beginning of May 1990 the Charity Finance Directors' Group (CFDG) launched a campaign with the slogan 'Charities Act 199?' in an attempt to highlight the issue.
- On 5 November 1991 the Charities Bill was finally published.

By this stage CFDG's campaign had been running for over eighteen months and putting that into context, the fact that the second reading in the House of Lords of the Bill was to be on 19 November and the debate was to be completed by 30 November it was, to say the least, somewhat rushed.

Strangely, all the discussion on the Bill took place in a committee of the House of Lords and it eventually went to the House of Commons in the final days just before the 1992 general election. The Charities Act 1992 was, therefore, the combination of several years' work and was subsequently consolidated into the Charities Act 1993.

Charities Acts 1992 and 1993

Following these Acts there was little immediate change in the way in which charity accounts were prepared and presented. However, since 1993 there have been considerable challenges for charity financial management in these areas. Why? Let's consider a few specific aspects.

Section 45 of the 1993 Act requires that every registered charity over a certain size should submit a full set of accounts, professionally audited or independently examined, to the Charity Commission within ten months of the end of its financial year, as laid down under section 43.

Accounting records, sufficient to show and explain the transactions in order to disclose with reasonable accuracy the financial position, have to be kept. These must show details of receipts and payments and of assets and liabilities and must be kept for at least six years after the end of the relevant financial year. (If the charity ceases to exist it can, with the approval of the Charity Commission, dispose of those accounting records.)

If the charity's gross income or total expenditure exceeded £250,000 for the relevant year, or either of the two previous years, the accounts must be audited. However, where the charity's gross income or total expenditure is less than £250,000 but more than £10,000 it can choose to have the accounts independently examined, provided that its governing document does not call for audit. If it does, it must have to have its accounts audited.

Section 43(3) of the Charities Act defines an independent examiner as 'an independent person who is reasonably believed by the trustees to have the requisite ability and practical experience to carry out a competent examination of the accounts'.

Some charities will have found for the first time that they had to produce an annual report. This again must be prepared and submitted to the Charity Commission within ten months of the end of the financial year. For most charities the report and the accounts are produced as one document.

Section 42 of the 1993 Act, which deals with the Annual Statement of Accounts, lays down that a charity's accounts must comply 'with such requirements as to its form and contents as may be prescribed by regulations made by the Secretary of State'. Section 47 states that members of the public have the right to request a copy of the charity's most recent report and accounts. The charity may charge a reasonable fee for this, but must supply the information within two months of receiving the request.

Section 42 states that where the gross income of the charity does not exceed £100,000 in any year, that charity need only prepare a receipts and payments account and a statement of assets and liabilities. For the purist accountant this is probably an anomaly. How can you have an asset/liabilities statement if you do not do accruals and only produce a receipts and payments account? The figure of £100,000 can be amended at any time by the order of the Secretary of State and where the figure is exceeded, full accrual-style accounts will have to be produced.

Statement of Recommended Practice (SORP) – Accounting by Charities

Following consultation, the Charities SORP was issued in October 1995 just before the regulations. Although it had no recommended start date the Charity Commission suggested that charities should adopt it as soon as possible. Accounting practice is such that to present a true and fair view, all standards, SORPs, etc., should be followed from the first accounting period following their production.

The 1995 SORP aim

The Charity Commission's prime aim and objective in publishing the SORP as set out in the document was:

> To help improve the quality of financial reporting by charities and to assist those who are responsible for the preparation of the charity's annual report and accounts. The intention is that these recommendations will reduce the current diversity in accounting practice and presentation.

Prescriptive approach

There was considerable debate about this approach, but it was felt to be the best way to proceed in order to provide simplicity and ensure consistency. One of the principal aims of accounting by charities must be to improve accountability and make comparisons by members of the public easier. It should also be borne in mind that the regulations, which are in themselves prescriptive, made much of the 1995 Charities SORP mandatory.

Report

The formal narrative statement was considerably expanded. This meant that the trustees' report must include information about the charity's objects, activities and achievements as well as a commentary on the financial position of the charity.

Figures

Arguably, the most radical change was the introduction of a 'statement of financial activities' (SOFA). This amalgamated the old income and expenditure account with the reconciliation and analysis of the movement of funds.

The assessment of the financial position of a charity is quite different from that of a business venture where profit is the main motive. A business raises capital, which it uses to generate profits. These are either distributed to those who contributed the capital, or retained in order to expand its profit-making capacity. A charity administers funds received for the purpose of its charitable objectives.

Investments

Investments held for long-term purposes used to be shown on the balance sheet at either cost or market value, however, the 1995 Charities SORP recommended that they be shown at market value under the general heading 'fixed assets' as a separate category. It went on to recommend that if investments were held as current assets, for example, where they were to be sold without reinvestment, then they should be valued at the lower of cost or net realisable value in the same way as other current assets.

As far as the treatment of gains and losses is concerned, the 1995 Charities SORP recommended a separate section, after the 'income and expenditure section', setting out in full both the realised and unrealised gains and losses.

Overhead costs

The definitions of fundraising and administration costs were amended and improved.

A new category was introduced so that much of what was reported under the heading of administration would, where appropriate, effectively be described as 'support costs', those costs incurred in respect of supporting direct charitable activities.

Summarised accounts

Where produced, these have to be approved formally by the trustees and accompanied by a statement from the auditors that they are consistent and accurate by reference to the full detailed accounts. Many charities issue publicity material containing accounts information, often in highly abbreviated and partly graphical or other pictorial form. All such information now had to follow the rules laid out in the 1995 Charities SORP.

Trading activities

The trading results of a charity's subsidiary(ies) have to be shown on the face of the SOFA, under the separate heading 'trading activities'. Where only the net income/expenditure is shown there has to be a full disclosure in the notes, giving the profit and loss account for each trading activity.

Branches

This change had a considerable effect on the way in which a number of charities produced their accounts. Accounting for branches was tightened and all branch transactions had to be reflected in the charity's own accounts, whether or not the funds were received by the parent charity by the year-end. Similarly, all assets and liabilities of the branch should be incorporated into the charity's own balance sheet.

Accounting concepts

The 1995 Charities SORP made explicit reference to accounting concepts. With the exception of smaller charities (gross income of less than £100,000), all charities have to prepare their accounts in accordance with the accounting concepts of an accrual basis, consistency, going concern and prudence. In the case of those smaller charities that are permitted by law to produce receipts and payments accounts, only the concept of consistency need apply.

'Light touch' approach

The effective removal from the SORP regime of the majority of charities occurred with the cut-off for the preparation of full accrual accounts set at £100,000 gross income per year. Furthermore, those charities with an annual income of less than £10,000, the so-called 'light touch' regime, need not have their accounts reviewed (independent examination/audit), nor submit them to the Charity Commission, unless they are specifically asked to do so.

Glossary

The 1995 Charities SORP includes a comprehensive glossary of definitions to enable readers unfamiliar with accounting terms to follow the document more easily.

Conclusion

The prescriptive approach taken in the 1995 Charities SORP undoubtedly changed the way in which many charities manage their finances and led to many more disclosures in the published accounts.

2   Regulatory Framework

Introduction

The accounting rules arising from Part VI of the Charities Act – the Charities (Accounts and Reports) Regulations 1995 – were published by the Home Office in October 1995, with a revised version published in October 2000. Significant points of interest arising from the regulations that are not covered by the SORP, except in so far as the regulations refer to it, are dealt with in this chapter.

Thresholds

The limits for unincorporated registered charities are:

ANNUAL GROSS INCOME	TYPE OF ACCOUNTS	TYPE OF REVIEW
Below £10,000	Receipts and payments	None
Above £10,000 but below £100,000	Receipts and payments	Independent examination
Above £100,000 but below £250,000	Accruals	Independent examination
Above £250,000	Accruals	Audit

In addition, charities with annual income of less than £1,000 and which do not have a permanent endowment need not register with the Charity Commission. Those charities with annual income of less than £10,000, the 'light touch' regime, need not submit a copy of their accounts to the Charity Commission unless they are specifically asked to do so. All registered charities with annual income in excess of £10,000 must submit a copy of their accounts to the Commission.

Annual returns

All registered charities must submit an annual return to the Commission. For the smaller charity the return is a fairly simple one to keep the record straight. Any charity can choose to impose upon itself more rigorous rules than the table sets out; for example, a charity with an income of less than £250,000 can elect to have its accounts audited rather than independently examined (see Chapter 13).

Independent examination is a less onerous form of scrutiny than audit, both in the terms of the depth of work that has to be carried out and the qualification necessary to undertake such work. The examiner is not required to form an opinion as to whether the accounts show a true and fair view, but based on the examination carried out, reports on whether specific matters have come to his or her attention.

However, many charities still require audit whatever their size because of their constitution/trust deed. This is a problem that the trustees will have to resolve if they want to make use of the independent examination procedures. Changes in company law as regards audit and audit exemption left some charities with a problem. In the table above the threshold for audit at £250,000 applies whether the charity is incorporated or unincorporated, but below that figure there could be a problem. Charities with an income in the range £10,000–£90,000 will require an independent examination if they are unincorporated, but will require no verification by an auditor or preparer of audit exemption reports if they are companies.

The table below sets out the situation with the inconsistent problem area in bold type. This matter remains unresolved and discussions

ANNUAL INCOME	UNINCORPORATED CHARITY		INCORPORATED CHARITY	
	AUDIT	INDEPENDENT EXAMINATION	AUDIT	AUDIT EXEMPTION REPORT
< £10,000	No	No	No	No
>£10,000–£90,000	No	**Yes**	No	**No**
>£90,000–£250,000	No	Yes	No	Yes
>£250,000	Yes	No	Yes	No

continue between the Charity Commission and the Department of Trade & Industry (DTI). The situation might have deteriorated following the DTI's proposal in early 1997 to abolish the 'accountant's report' for businesses with turnover between £90,000 and £350,000 (the threshold for audit for non-charitable companies). As reported in *Accountancy Age* (30 January 1997), this would have created a loophole for unscrupulous individuals to carry out fraud under the cover of charitable companies. Fortunately, the DTI listened to the Charity Commission and to the charity sector generally and agreed not only to exempt charities from this new ruling, but also to look at ways of reviewing the existing anomaly. As the official report stated:

> 'The current arrangements will be retained for those charities which have chosen to incorporate, pending an *early consultatio*n on options for harmonisation of the financial reporting requirements under charities legislation on the one hand and companies legislation on the other.'

(The italics are added as the report was issued early in 1997.) One would hope that as a result of the revised SORP and the review of the regulations carried out by the Charity Commission this problem would finally have been sorted out. All charitable companies will have to produce their accounts on the accruals basis and comply with company law regulations (see further Chapter 11).

October 2000 revisions

In following the SORP the regulations on annual reports section is probably somewhat over-detailed. However, the reports of a charity whose gross income does not exceed £100,000 may be a brief summary of the main activities and achievements of the charity during the year in relation to its objects and not the fuller version previously recommended. Any remuneration paid to trustees or persons connected with the charity must be shown in the notes to the accounts (Part IV, paragraph 1(c)) and now like the SORP (revised 2000) there is a requirement to show the number of employees within set salary bands of £10,000 from a base of £50,000 upwards.

Some of the recommended changes to the SORP required changes to the regulations. The Home Office therefore issued for discussion Draft Regulations on Charity Accounts and Reports on 22 February 2000.

Comments on these Draft Regulations had to be submitted by 30 April 2000 to the Charity Commission. The consultation document was very technical, but in summary it covered:

- whether to raise the annual income threshold for simpler arrangements for preparing annual reports and accounts from £100,000 to £250,000;
- how best to cover Governance arrangements and investment and reserves policies and practices in the Annual Report, at least for larger charities;
- how to make the detailed analysis in the accounts of incoming resources less prescriptive;
- how to revise the expenditure analysis to bring it in line with the revised SORP;
- how to cover historic or inalienable assets;
- how to revise the rules on related party transactions in the light of a recent accounting standard and the revised SORP;
- how to make various other minor and technical changes to maintain consistency with the revised SORP;
- whether to make a minor amendment on the rules on accounts scrutiny to allow the Charity Commission to give a dispensation at an earlier stage;
- where exactly to draw the boundary of the special accounting regime for Common Deposit Funds and non-pooling scheme Common Investment Funds;
- how to carry out technical updating of the rules for registered social landlords and certain designated education institutions, including making explicit that the accounts for these bodies must give a true and fair view; and
- whether provision needed to be made for any additional classes of charity to be allowed to treat accounts prepared under some other statutory accounting regime as also being their accounts for the purposes of the charity accounting regime; and whether that treatment should be conditional on the alternative accounts giving a true and fair view.

The Charities (Accounts and Reports) Regulations 2000 were laid before Parliament on 25 October 2000 as SI 2000, No. 2868. The Regulations came into force on 15 November 2000 for statements of accounts prepared by the charity trustees of a charity in respect of the financial year that began on or after 1 January 2001. If the trustees wished, earlier adoption could have been undertaken, and had to be if the trustees had not either approved the accounts of the charity or authorised the signing of the annual report for accounts ended before that date by 15 November 2000. The Regulations follow very closely the Statement of Recommended Practice and, in particular, have dealt with all the issues raised above. (See further Chapter 3.)

A copy of the revised Regulations is available from HMSO or on their website at <www.hmso.gov.uk>.

3   The Statement of Recommended Practice (SORP)

Introduction

This chapter looks in some detail at the revision of the October 1995 SORP, which was discussed in Chapter 1. In September 1998, the Charity Commission launched a review of the SORP and charities and those interested had until 7 December 1998 to submit their comments and views. The major points on which the Charity Commission requested opinions were:

- Editorial.
- Consolidation, branches and combined charities.
- Trading.
- Accruals accounting for incoming resources.
- Expenditure classifications.
- Measurement and valuation principles.
- Summary income and expenditure account and summary accounts.
- Fund accounting.
- Reserves.

Charity Commission SORP consultation – review of comments

In spring 1999 the Charity Commission produced a short report drawing together all the comments they had received. A committee was appointed to review the operation of the Charities SORP in light of the comments received.

Whilst it was agreed that fundamental changes were not required, a view was expressed that certain areas of the SORP needed clarification and that ambiguities should be removed, but that the SORP should not be amended to the detriment of the majority just to please a small minority!

The changes

The 2000 Charities SORP has been completely rewritten, although there are no major changes to the structure of the accounts, nor are there any requirements that should be regarded as difficult. The Charity Commission makes the point that whilst the document is regarded as recommended best practice, charities may provide additional information in order to give the reader an improved view of the activities and achievements of the charity concerned.

Unfortunately, because of the diversity of the sector, in terms of size, structure and activity, this revised SORP has increased in length. In addition, certain sections have been included at the specific request of charities to deal with special situations, although there are few, if any charities, to which all parts of the SORP will apply. Charities should therefore ignore the sections that do not apply to them. As it is not possible – or indeed desirable – to be prescriptive on every issue, those who prepare and review charity accounts will, as ever, need to exercise their judgement in certain areas.

The revised SORP is principally a guide for those who prepare, audit or examine charity accounts. It is written in accounting language and as a result may not be easily understood by those with little or no knowledge of accounting principles and standards. However, as trustees are ultimately responsible for the resources and finances of their charity as they are reflected in the accounts, those trustees with little or no knowledge of accounting matters will need to seek reassurance on these matters from colleagues, staff or professional advisers.

All the anomalies have been removed, particularly those relating to consolidation, the need for a separate income and expenditure account and trading activities. As long ago as September 1997 a former Charity Commissioner, John Bonds, is on record as agreeing in respect of accounting for investment gains and losses that:

> 'If in such a case a charity decides to disclose total investment gains/losses (both realised and unrealised) under one heading 'net investment gains/losses' on the Statement of Financial Activities, the Charity Commission will not raise any objections.'

Therefore, this change has been made to the SORP. However, the most significant change is in the name of the document. In both the 1988 and 1995 versions it was 'Accounting by Charities'. In the 2000 version it is

'Accounting and Reporting by Charities'. This is a deliberate attempt by the Charity Commission to ensure that more emphasis is placed by charities and their trustees on the production of the Trustees' Report.

One issue that many would very much like to have seen resolved is that of the inherent inconsistencies between the accounting treatment required by a charitable company and that of an unincorporated charity. These in particular relate to the conflicts between the Companies Act 1985 and the Charities Act 1993 (see further Chapter 11). There are also inconsistencies between the reporting thresholds and the need for audit and in areas such as the auditors' duty of whistle-blowing which, under the 1993 Charities Act, affects unincorporated charities only (see further Chapter 13).

What is new?

In the Trustees' Annual Report, trustees are asked to comment on their reserves (the policy, the level and the justification), their investment and grant-making policies and their internal controls (see further Chapter 4). There is now very detailed cross-referencing to Statements of Standard Accounting Practice (SSAPs) and Financial Reporting Standards (FRSs) and an appendix which is a summary of all existing accounting standards showing their application to charities (see further Chapter 6).

A new section has been included on the impairment of fixed assets following the publication of FRS11. This, however, is unlikely to apply to many charities (see further Chapter 6). Sub-sections dealing with transactions with trustees (including their expenses) and connected persons have been included, which certainly answers all the queries received in response to the Charity Commission request of September 1997 (see further Chapter 8).

Also new is a very detailed and self-explanatory section dealing with charitable companies, which should resolve all the anomalies and problems flowing from the 1995 Charities SORP (see further Chapter 11). For smaller charities it is proposed that the threshold for reporting resources expended as set out in the SORP should be increased from £100,000 to £250,000 a year (see further Chapter 12).

Revised/extended

Accounting for separate funds has been explained in much more detail (see further Chapter 3).

The precise requirements for narrative information (as distinct from legal and administrative information) in the Trustees' Annual Report have been reduced in order to encourage charities to expand on their activities rather than answer a series of questions (see further Chapter 4).

In the Statement of Financial Activities (SOFA) the presentation of incoming resources and resources expended has been altered to provide a more logical layout to fit in with the way in which charities handle their transactions and prepare their accounts. Incoming resources and resources expended of a similar nature will be grouped together and will be consolidated where there are subsidiary undertakings.

The rules for recognising incoming resources have been restated, with the emphasis now on three factors: entitlement, certainty and measurement. The information on accounting for legacies has been extended to deal more clearly with the thorny issue of what to disclose, when to disclose and the accrual situation (see further Chapter 5).

The guidance in relation to dealing with intangible income and donations in kind – for example, donated facilities, beneficial loan arrangements, donated services or services from volunteers – have been clarified. They now need be recorded only where another party is bearing the financial cost of those resources as supplied, and the benefit is quantifiable and measurable (see further Chapter 5).

The section on trading has been completely revised and brought up to date. Trading is now more accurately defined as 'operating activities' using accounting rather than taxation rules. All income from non-charitable trading is now to be combined under one heading (see further Chapter 5).

The requirements for disclosing grants are set out more fully, with the emphasis on providing the analysis and explanation necessary to understand how the grants made by a charity relate to its objects. Disclosure is required when grants total at least £250,000 in the year, or 5 per cent of total resources expended (see further Chapter 5).

The definition of fundraising costs has been improved and replaced by the more correct terminology 'costs of generating funds'. Investment management fees can be included under 'costs of generating funds' provided that they are disclosed separately in the notes to the accounts. This requirement to disclose also applies to all material items of cost under this heading (see further Chapter 5).

The balance sheet section is the area where the most radical changes have taken place. However, they are only radical to the extent that there is a considerable extension from what was required under the 1995 Charities SORP. This has been done to take account of FRS11, 12 and 15, which deal with 'Impairment of Fixed Assets and Goodwill', 'Provisions, Contingent Liabilities and Contingent Assets' and 'Tangible Fixed Assets', respectively. These three FRSs were issued after the 1995 Charities SORP which therefore needed to be updated to take account of them (see further Chapter 6).

The section on the Cash flow Statement has been amended and updated to take account of FRS1, which was revised in 1996 after the publication of the 1995 Charities SORP (see further Chapter 7). The consolidation of subsidiary undertakings has been expanded to replace the previous section on consolidation and should overcome the problems previously faced (see further Chapter 10). The section on smaller charities has been extended and a greater emphasis placed on accounting aspects (see further Chapter 12).

Charity Commission aim

All charity trustees have a duty to keep proper accounting records for their charity, which set out and explain all the charity's transactions. The SORP effectively provides guidance on how this should be done annually in relation to the resources entrusted to the charity and the activities it has undertaken. The SORP applies to all charities regardless of their size, constitution or complexity, except in those cases where a more specialised SORP applies, for example for registered social landlords.

The Charity Commission expects charities to comply fully with this or any other applicable SORP. Where they do not the charity's accounts should identify this and provide a full explanation. Where the Charity Commission feels that the explanation is unsatisfactory or no explanation is given the matter may be raised with the charity concerned and, in exceptional circumstances, the Charity Commission may institute an enquiry.

Quite clearly, the Charity Commission's objective in publishing these recommendations is to improve the quality of financial reporting by charities and to assist those who are responsible for the preparation of the charity's Annual Report and Accounts. The intention is that these recom mendations will reduce the diversity in accounting practice and presentation. In all but exceptional circumstances charities preparing accrual accounts should follow this SORP in order for their accounts to give a true and fair view. However, depending upon the size and complexity of a charity's operation, the impact of the SORP will be different and to help smaller charities in particular the Charity Commission produces a range of simplified guidance.

General principles

Accounts intending a true and fair view must be prepared on the going concern assumption and the accruals concept, and provide information that is relevant, reliable, comparable and understandable. Where charities can choose to prepare receipts and payments accounts the information must be comparable. This is normally achieved through the application of consistent policies. In meeting the obligation to prepare accounts that show a true and fair view, consideration has to be given to the standards laid down in Statements of Standard Accounting Practice (SSAPs), Financial Reporting Standards (FRSs) and Urgent Issues Task Force Abstracts (UITFs) issued or adopted by the Accounting Standards Board which are relevant to the charity's circumstances and accounts. The revised SORP provides guidance and interpretation of the most suitable application of accounting standards for charities, but it is supplementary to those standards and does not repeat all of their requirements.

The main purpose of the Statement of Financial Activities (SOFA) is to give an overall view of the total incoming resources during the year and how they have been spent, with the balance sheet showing the overall financial position at the year-end. There are additional requirements for charities that have to account for more than one fund under their control. The accounts should provide a summary of the main funds, differentiating in particular between the unrestricted income funds, restricted income funds and endowment funds. The columnar format of the SOFA is designed to achieve this. Charities need to account for the proper administration of the individual funds in accordance with their respective terms of trust, and accounting records must be kept in a way that adequately separates transactions between different funds. Some charities may hold one or more restricted funds, some of which may be permanent or expendable endowment funds. Depending on the materiality of each, the

notes to the accounts should group the restricted funds under one or
more headings.

Unrestricted income funds

Unrestricted income funds (also known as general funds) are expendable
at the discretion of the trustees in furtherance of the objects of the charity.

Designated funds

Where part of an unrestricted fund is earmarked for a particular project it
may be described as designated as a separate fund. However, that designation has an administrative purpose only and does not legally restrict
the trustees' discretion to apply the fund. In other words, trustees retain
the right to use those funds in furtherance of the objects of the charity.

Restricted funds

Restricted funds are subject to specific trusts declared by the donor(s), or
with their authority (for example, in a public appeal). They can be used
only for the purposes for which they are given. Restricted funds may be
restricted income funds that are expendable in furtherance of some
particular aspects of the objects of the charity; or they may be capital
funds, where the assets are required to be invested, or retained for actual
use.

Endowment funds

A fund where there is no power to convert the capital into income is
known as a permanent endowment fund and must generally be held
indefinitely. This concept of 'permanence' does not necessarily mean that
the assets held in the endowment fund cannot be exchanged; nor does it
mean that they are incapable of depreciation or loss. What it does mean is
that the permanent endowment fund cannot be used as if it were income.

Fund accounting

The treatment of movements of funds should not be affected by the type
of fund involved. This means, for example, that restricted and
unrestricted incoming resources receivable at the same time should be

accounted for in the SOFA at the same time. This should also reflect the principal movements between the opening and closing balances on all the funds of the charity. The SOFA should be analysed between unrestricted income funds, restricted funds and endowment funds with permanent and expendable combined (see further Chapter 5).

The notes to the accounts should provide information on the structure of the charity's funds so as to disclose fund balances and the reasons for them differentiating between unrestricted income funds (general and designated), restricted income funds, permanent and expendable endowment as well as identifying any material individual funds within them. In particular, the assets and liabilities representing each type of fund of the charity should be clearly summarised and analysed between those funds (see further Chapter 8).

The restrictions imposed upon each fund and details of how they have arisen, along with the purpose, should be stated in the notes. This disclosure should indicate whether or not sufficient resources are held in an appropriate form to enable each fund to be used in accordance with any restrictions. Any funds in deficit should always be separately disclosed and an explanation given in the Trustees' Annual Report. Additionally, explanations should be provided for any unusual movement in any of the funds and material transfers between different funds and allocations to designated funds should be separately disclosed without netting off.

Separate sets of statements may, if required, be produced for each major fund linked to a summary. It is for the trustees to decide on the most suitable form of presentation, bearing in mind the complexity of the funds structure and the need to avoid confusion between the movements on the various funds.

Branches

Many charities have organisations that conduct activities at local levels. These organisations are known under various headings such as supporter groups, branches, friends or affiliates. The Charities SORP uses the term 'branch' to denote an entity that:

- may be part of the administrative machinery of the main charity; or
- is a separate legal entity that is administered by or on behalf of the main charity. The branch's funds are held for the specific purpose of

the main charity and the main charity can exert 'a substantial degree of influence' over the branch.

Where the SORP views branches as non-autonomous entities, they must be accounted for in full in the accounts of the main charity. Paragraph 53 states that all branch transactions should be accounted for gross and all assets and liabilities of the local branch should be included in the main accounts. However, separate legal entities that may be known as branches but which do not fall within the definition of a branch should prepare their own annual report and accounts and, if they are connected to charities, the relationship should be explained in the Trustees' Report.

Where the branch is not a separate legal entity and its accounts have then formed part of the accounts of the reporting charity it may well be in the interests of local supporters and beneficiaries for additional accounts to be prepared covering only that branch.

Any funds raised by a branch for the general purposes of the parent charity will be accounted for as unrestricted funds in the accounts of the parent charity. However, funds raised by a branch for the specific purposes of the parent charity will need to be accounted for as restricted funds in the parent charity's accounts. Conversely, funds held for the general purposes of a branch, which is a separate charity, would usually be accounted for as restricted funds in the accounts of the main charity.

Timing

The Charity Commission committee to review the SORP completed its work in June 2000 and clearance from the Accounting Standards Board was obtained in July 2000. The revised SORP was published in October 2000 and is effective for accounting periods that began on or after 1 January 2001. *The SORP, a Guide to the Changes* (CC62), *Charity Accounts 2001: The Framework* (CC61) an introductory accounts aimed specifically at non-accountants, a booklet containing a series of example reports and accounts (CC66) and other publications issued following the Revised SORP are available on the Charity Commission's website (www.charity-commission.gov.uk) or by phoning the publications order line on 01823 345427.

4   Trustees' Annual Report

Introduction

The charity world has frequently expressed its accountability and measured its effectiveness in purely financial terms. However, this approach is only part of the picture and cash is often a poor proxy for value. Charity accounts too rarely contain the qualitative information essential for a full understanding of the figures. The information that is needed is not how much has been spent, but how much has been achieved in relation to the issues being addressed and meeting the charity's objectives. The Trustees' Report, along with the sometimes glossy annual review, can successfully carry out this function.

Stakeholders need to know how the charity is succeeding in its aim to achieve its particular objectives. Otherwise, there will be a break in the special relationship between the stakeholders and the charity, even in cases where the stakeholders want to support the objectives of the organisation. In fact, the charity that is not in some way accountable and cannot satisfy the various stakeholders' different requirements will be in some difficulty (see further below).

It is essential that the Trustees' Report provides basic information relating to the charity, its trustees and officers, as well as a concise but comprehensive review of the charity's activities. The Trustees' Report should, therefore, provide detailed information that ties in with the expenditure headings in the accounts that follow. It should also provide other qualitative, non-financial indicators, as ChildLine do by showing the number of children counselled.

Charities Act 1993

Section 45 of the Charities Act 1993 makes it quite clear that:

> 'The charity trustees of a charity should prepare in respect of each financial year of the charity an annual report containing:
>> a   such a report by the trustees on the activities of the charity during that year; and

   b   such other information relating to the charity or to its trustees or offices; as may be prescribed by regulations made by the Secretary of State.'

Regulations

The requirements in relation to the annual report are set out in the 2000 Regulation 7(3) as follows:

'a in the case of any financial year of a charity in which neither its gross income nor its total expenditure exceeds £250,000, a brief summary of the main activities and achievements of the charity during the year;

b in the case of any financial year of a charity in which its gross income exceeds £250,000: –

   i   be a review of all activities, including –

      aa material transactions, significant developments and achievements of the charity during the year in relation to its objects;

      bb any significant changes in those activities during the year;

      cc any important events effecting those activities that have occurred since the end of the year and any likely future developments in those activities; and

      dd where any fund of the charity was in deficit at the beginning of the financial year, the steps taken by the charity trustees to eliminate that deficit; and

   ii contain a statement as to whether the charity trustees have given consideration to –

      aa the major risks to which the charity is exposed; and

      bb systems designed to mitigate those risks; and

c in either case, be dated and signed by one or more of the charity trustees, each of whom has been authorised to do so.'

SORP

The 1995 SORP recommended that the formal narrative statement be considerably expanded. This meant that the Trustees' Report had to include information about the charity's objects, activities and achievements, as well as a commentary on the financial position of the charity. However, despite best endeavours, this did not appear to be happening, so the revised 2000 SORP reinforced the position by restating the requirements.

The detail for the narrative information has been reduced in order to encourage charities to expand their activities and achievement of their objectives. In particular, trustees are asked to report on their reserves (the policy, the level and the justification) and where applicable their investment and grant-making policies, as well as the effectiveness of their fundraising activities. Trustees should also provide a statement confirming that the major risks to which the charity is exposed have been reviewed and systems established to minimise those risks (SORP, paragraphs 26–9).

Of particular interest to all charity trustees is this new requirement for a statement relative to risks the charity faces. It is important to recognise that this does not refer to financial risks only – hence, legal and operational matters must also be considered. This requirement reflects the reporting now required by listed companies following the publication of the Turnbull Report in 1999.

To paraphrase the SORP, paragraph 26, it is the trustees' responsibility to prepare in respect of each financial year accounts and notes which comply with the SORP and a report setting out the narrative information required at paragraph 31. This report should describe what the charity is trying to do and how it is achieving its objectives. For those charities that are incorporated, and to avoid duplication, the trustees/directors should ensure that their annual report as trustees includes all those matters that are required to be included in the Statutory Directors' Report.

Trustees are advised to include any additional information that they are required by law to report and they should confirm that the accounts comply with the current legal requirements, the requirements of the charity's governing document and the requirements of the revised SORP. The report and accounts have to be approved by the trustees acting together according to their governing document. Both the report and the accounts should be signed by at least one of the trustees who has been authorised to do so by the trustee board. The date of approval needs to be given.

Any trustee who considers that the report and/or accounts should not be approved, or should not have been approved, should report this matter to the Charity Commission along with any concern which they were unable to resolve with their fellow trustees.

Whenever a full set of accounts is distributed by the charity it must have attached to it the Trustees' Annual Report together with the audit/independent report on the accounts. To summarise the Trustees' Annual Report should:

- explain the objects of the charity;
- provide a description of the organisational structure of the charity;
- explain how decisions are made;
- include a statement regarding the relationship between the charity and related parties/other charities with which it cooperates;
- provide a review of the activities of the charity;
- include a statement of the charity's policies, for example, on reserves, investments and grant-making;
- where funds are in deficit provide an explanation of why they are in deficit and the action that has been taken;
- include a statement confirming that major risks to which the charity is exposed have been reviewed and systems have been established to minimise those risks.

A statement should be included setting out the legal and administrative details either as part of the report or as a separate section in the report and accounts (SORP, paragraph 30). These include such things as the full name of the charity, a list of the trustees and the method of appointment/election, the address of the principal office, the names and addresses of principal advisers, an indication of the nature of the governing document, details of specific restrictions and a summary of any specific investment powers.

It is important that trustees, when preparing the Trustees' Report, appreciate the balance between clarity and brevity. Some reports are too long and detailed and are therefore not read, whilst others are so short that they may raise more questions than they answer and do not meet the minimum requirements. As we have seen, the regulations under the Charities Act 1993 stipulate the minimum requirement of the annual Trustees' Report whilst the SORP itself provides further recommendations.

Stakeholder reporting

The debate about stakeholders and stewardship in the charity world has been live for some considerable time but it effectively started to come to a head with the publication of the draft revised SORP 2, in 1993.

The Charity Commission committee spent some considerable time debating the issue of stakeholders, in particular in relation to the audience for the accounts for which it was effectively producing the Charities SORP. As a result, no firm conclusions were reached other than a consensus that the accounts were not being produced solely for the benefit of the Charity Commission. This decision probably resulted in the Commission requiring auditors and independent examiners to 'whistle-blow'.

However, the topic had had a good airing even earlier, in 1991, in the House of Lords, during the debate on the Charities Bill. Considerable hot air was expanded at that time on precisely who were the recipients of charity reports and accounts. We do need to remember that this subject is not just about the financial affairs of charities. It is about reporting generally.

All those with an involvement in charity, commonly described as stakeholders – whether donors, beneficiaries, trustees, employees, creditors, grantees, etc. – have the right to expect that the resources entrusted to a charity are being used cost-effectively and efficiently. It must, therefore, be part of the reporting procedure to ensure that this happens.

It is probably sensible to define what is meant by stakeholders. Put very simply, it is anyone with any interest whatsoever in the particular charity. This is what makes stakeholder reporting so difficult – very different perhaps from the corporate sector and even the public sector. Quite clearly, the tighter you define stakeholders the easier the reporting becomes.

Ian Bruce, in his excellent book *Successful Charity Marketing: Meeting Need* (ICSA Publishing, second edition 1998), makes the point that stakeholders are a 'target group of people who are crucial to a charity marketing approach'. He goes on, however, to define stakeholders as just one of four classes of charity customer (the other three being beneficiaries, supporters and regulators). However, these are probably only really classes of stakeholders rather than a stakeholder being a class of charity customer. This shows the vagaries of opinion in the charity world.

By contrast, David Wise, in his first-class book *Performance Measurement for Charities* (ICSA Publishing, 1995), seems to agree with the earlier definition of stakeholders, and not with that of Ian Bruce, when he makes the point:

'Businesses exist for the benefit of their shareholders. Charities exist for the benefit of their beneficiaries. But, in both cases it is recognised that regard must be paid to other stakeholders if the primary stakeholder interests are to be best served.'

Whether or not the beneficiaries, supporters, regulators or customers are stakeholders is probably irrelevant. What is important is that whatever definition is accepted one does need to report to all these groups.

Indeed, all charity accounts and reports do have a constant and well-informed readership in the Charity Commission, Inland Revenue and HM Customs & Excise (particularly in the latter two cases in Scotland and Northern Ireland). All these bodies demand copies of financial statements and can, and do, demand further explanation of any matters they find unclear. Charity trustees, therefore, may find it useful to prepare the Trustees' Report as if it were addressed to these officials in the first instance.

Reporting by charities has improved tremendously over the last few years as individual charities have attempted to raise their profiles. This must be encouraged. Charities need to be far more open about their activities, for example by explaining how they are achieving their objectives.

The SORP goes to great lengths to set out the sort of information that it wishes to see in the trustees' annual report. As David Wise puts it:

'Strategic review of performance should involve a balanced view of stakeholder perspectives and activities within the charity.'

Research into the financial reporting by charities often highlights the problem of stakeholder reporting which is perceived to be peculiar to the charity world, but which is becoming less so as more and more companies find that they too need to take account of their customers, suppliers, staff, etc. One such research project carried out at the Plymouth Business School concluded that:

'The purpose of a charity's report and accounts should serve as a medium between the charity and the public. Donors (potential or otherwise) should be properly informed about the position of a charity. A charity's annual report and accounts are therefore public documents and should not require professional skills to examine them (i.e. those of a professional accountant).'

This is a very sensible and logical conclusion as too often the only public reporting done by a charity is in its annual report and accounts which, because of the way in which they are presented, are often meaningless to all but the very informed, qualified reader. Here, charities could take a leaf out of the corporate world's book. Many corporate accounts have become much more informative and far easier to read than the average set of charity accounts.

The only thing that is certain is that there can be no firm conclusions on the topic of stakeholder reporting. All charities must continue to improve their reporting to all those who have an interest in the operation of the charity, not just to meet legal requirements, but to ensure their continued survival.

Example

The following example of a trustee report was prepared by the author as a member of The Charity Accounting Review Committee (1999/2000) for the publication *SORP 2000: Example Reports and Accounts* (CC66, November 2000).

Example 4.1

ARTS THEATRE TRUST

Legal and Administrative Information

The Charity is registered and is a company limited by guarantee governed by its memorandum and articles of association. Charity number: 1234567. Company number 89101112.

Directors/Trustees:
The Directors of the charitable company (the Charity) are its trustees for the purposes of charitable law and throughout this report are collectively referred to as the trustees. Five trustees from BF Borough Council and three trustees from B Town Council are nominated by the respective Councils. As set out in the Articles of Association the trustee from N Arts is their Chairman. Two trustees are elected annually by the members attending the AGM and serve for a period of two years. These trustees have the power to co-opt up to two further members to fill specialist roles. The trustees serving during the year and since the year end were as follows:

BF Borough Council	B Town Council
F. A. Brown	E. R. Allsop
A. D. S. Jones	E. M. Barrett
W. M. Smith	E. P. Cross (resigned 14 June 2001)
M. J. Young	C. Norfolk (appointed 15 June 2001)
C. I. West	

N Arts – Nominated Chairman	Elected members
S. A. Bloggs (appointed 10 July 2000)	B. Bates
M. L. King (resigned 10 July 2000)	D. Evans
S. Richards	
E. Towns	

Co-opted member
D. East

Secretary and registered office
ATC Park, Anytown Town, Bshire, BX56 7SG

Auditors
CEP & Co, 23 High Street, Anytown, Bshire, BX56 4TP

Bankers
Cruffs Bank plc, 10 High Street, Anytown, Bshire, BX56 1SG

Solicitors
Backhouse & Co, 15 Low Road, Anytown, Bshire, BX56 3PS

ARTS THEATRE TRUST LIMITED

Report of the Trustees for the year ended 31 March 2001

Trustees are pleased to submit their report and accounts for the year ended 31 March 2001.

Legal and administrative information set out on page 1 forms part of this report. The financial statements comply with current statutory requirements, the Memorandum and Articles of Association and the Statement of Recommended Practice – Accounting and Reporting by Charities.

Objects of the charity
The objects of the charity are to advance the education of the public in all aspects of dramatic art and the development of public appreciation of such art by the provision of a theatre and the presentation of public performances. The theatre contributes to the quality of life of the people of BF Borough and beyond, by expanding their horizons through the provision of exciting, challenging and accessible professional and community arts events. The principal activities continued to relate to the promotion and fostering of artistic knowledge and appreciation of the arts by the provision of facilities for the education and entertainment of the public in the fields of art, craft, music and drama. To achieve this the charity:

- Offers opportunities for a broad range of people to get involved in arts activity exploring their own creative powers.

- Provides facilities for amateur and professional artists to develop. Groups in the Borough are given discounted rates for hire of space and access to professional advice.
- Concentrates on involving young people in the arts to help encourage a culture in which different age ranges play a complementary part.
- Celebrates the diversity of cultures in our society by programming presentations by, and with artists of different cultural backgrounds.
- Presents a broad range of arts work.

Organisation
The Charity is administered by a board of fifteen members, which meets quarterly. There are sub-committees covering development, membership, finance and audit. A Chief Executive is appointed by the board to manage the day-to-day operations of the Charity.

Investment powers
Under the Memorandum and Articles of Association, the charity has the power to make any investments which the trustees see fit.

Related parties
The Trust has a very close relationship with BF Borough Council, B Town Council and N Arts, a charity, all of which nominate trustees and provide funding to enable the trust to carry out its charitable objectives (see further Note 20).

The Trust also co-operates with a number of local arts charities and not-for-profit organisations to provide them with subsidised accommodation and facilities.

Review of activities and future developments
On 25 November 2000 the Trust celebrated fifty years of successful operation at ATC Park.

The end of the year saw an excellent financial result based on strong financial management. Costs were contained within budget and income budgets were exceeded in both the arts and trading areas. Artistic quality was high in the programme of events, courses, performances and work-shops that appealed to a wide range of customers. The surplus of income over expenditure for the year ending 2001 was £78,000 (2000, £27,000).

Attendances at the theatre increased from 78,000 in the year ending 31 March 2000 to over 85,000 in the year ended 31 March 2001. Eighteen different performances were carried out and over one hundred different workshops were put on, all of which were very well attended.

During the year, the trustees submitted an application to the Arts Council of England National Lottery Capital Programme, following a feasibility study carried out with funding from the Arts Council of England, for £500,000 to refurbish and develop the site at ATC Park. An additional submission was made to BF Borough Council requesting £500,000 towards the scheme which was approved subject to the successful outcome of our bid to the National Lottery Capital Programme.

The main elements of the scheme will enable the charity to expand our programmes for young people and the promotion of cultural diversity, allowing all our programmes and activities to be delivered with increasing access to new media such as the Internet. The potential impact of this development is explained further in the section below on reserves policy and risk management.

The charity's wholly owned subsidiary company, HTC Limited, undertook its first full year of operating the commercial trading activities run at the Park. Total profits of £223,000 (2000, £16,000) from HTC were gifted to the charity. The trustees are pleased with the commercial success of this venture which allows additional funds to be generated to meet our charitable objectives.

The staff deserve credit and praise for their skilful and enthusiastic efforts to provide a successful service to a growing broad range of customers.

Reserves policy and risk management

In 1999 the Trustees carried out a detailed review of the charities' activities and produced a comprehensive strategic plan setting out the major opportunities available to the charity and the risks to which it is exposed. The trustees monitor progress against the strategic objectives set out in the plan at each quarterly meeting and a comprehensive review of the plan is carried out annually. As part of this process, the trustees have implemented a risk management strategy that comprises:

- An annual review of the risks that the charity may face;
- The establishment of systems and procedures to mitigate those risks identified in the plan; and
- The implementation of procedures designed to minimise any potential impact on the charity should any of those risks materialise.

The strategic plan focused the trustees on the need to refurbish and develop our ATC Park site further, resulting in the application for funding mentioned previously. A successful outcome is dependent on the charity meeting the challenges such a major project presents and managing our finances prudently.

The trustees have forecast the level of free reserves (that is those funds not tied up in fixed assets, and designated and restricted funds). The charity will require to sustain its operations over the period when it is anticipated that some of the income generating activities may be curtailed temporarily whilst the anticipated project will be carried out. The trustees consider that the most appropriate level of free reserves at 31 March 2001 would be £475,000 reducing to £325,000 at 31 March 2002. The actual free reserves at 31 March 2001 were £381,000 which is

£94,000 short of our target figure. Whilst the current level of reserves may prove sufficient, it is the trustees view that it is prudent to ensure that there are sufficient free reserves to provide financial flexibility over the course of the forthcoming challenges.

The trustees have therefore planned a new fundraising strategy concentrating on raising funds from our existing audiences and customers of our wholly-owned trading subsidiary, HTC Limited, with a view to increasing our free reserves to the appropriate level. The trustees will closely monitor this initiative against the budgets that have been set. As part of the feasibility study we have shared our plans with our bankers, Cruffs Bank Plc, which has indicated that it will provide support in order to see our planned development come to fruition.

Trustees' responsibilities in relation to the financial statements

Company law requires the board to prepare accounts that give a true and fair view of the state of affairs of the charity at the end of the financial year and of its surplus or deficit for the financial year. In doing so the trustees are required to:

- select suitable accounting policies and then apply them consistently;
- make judgements and estimates that are reasonable and prudent; and
- prepare the financial statements on the going concern basis unless it is inappropriate to presume that the company will continue in business.

The trustees are responsible for maintaining proper accounting records which disclose with reasonable accuracy at any time the financial position of the charity and enables it to ensure that the accounts comply with the Companies Act 1985. The trustees are also responsible for safeguarding the assets of the charity and hence for taking reasonable steps for the prevention and detection of fraud and other irregularities.

Auditors

A resolution will be proposed at the Annual General Meeting that CEP & Co be re-appointed as auditors to the charity for the ensuing year.

By order of the trustees

S. A. Bloggs (Chairman)

13 June 2001

5   Statement of Financial Activities (SOFA)

Introduction

The traditional income and expenditure account had for some time led to complaints that it did not reflect or fully explain all the financial activities of the charity. Therefore, it was considered that the very nature of the raising and using of charity resources required a different approach from that of the business community.

Charities do not have shareholders, even those that are companies, so matters such as distributing or retaining profit do not arise. Moreover, those who provide the resources for charities do not usually expect a monetary return on their donations, but more of a warm glow! However, the users of a charity's financial statements do need to be able to assess the services that the charity is providing, primarily through its charitable expenditure and its ability to continue to provide those services.

The evolution of the Statement of Financial Activities (SOFA)

The accounts should show how the trustees have carried out their duties and ensured that their responsibilities have been met during the year. Whilst it may be that the bottom line, surplus or deficit, provides some of this information, any presentation that focuses only on the bottom line tends to ignore the fundamental differences between accounting for charities and accounting for the business sector.

What is the bottom line when there is in effect no bottom line?

Charities, except those that are effectively trading, are not usually in the business of directly matching income and expenditure. Therefore, they are not working towards a particular year-end date. In other words, to place undue emphasis on the bottom line at a particular point in time can be misleading, as income and expenditure in any one period are not often directly linked. Grants received this year, for example, may be for projects to be carried out next year – or indeed over a number of years.

Furthermore, the traditional income and expenditure account, with its distinction between revenue and capital, does not always explain adequately a charity's activities. Businesses primarily invest in fixed assets to generate future profits whilst a charity may be investing in fixed assets as part of its charitable activity (primary purpose) – for example, equipping a cancer research laboratory, building an old people's home, acquiring lifeboats, building kennels. This difference is extremely important to certain charities where a significant proportion of their annual expenditure is of a capital nature.

In any particular year a charity may use part of its income to purchase fixed assets for its charitable activities and, since this expenditure is of a capital nature, it will not be shown in the income and expenditure account. This could lead to a surplus on the income and expenditure account and give a misleading impression. Unfortunately, the SOFA still does not include capital expenditure, whether of a charitable or other nature, and so judging the charity on the bottom line criterion will continue to be misleading in those circumstances where there is significant charitable objective spending of a capital nature.

Disclosures

Foremost amongst the recommendations of the earliest Charity SORP was the introduction of the statement of financial activities (SOFA). This is a way of showing in summary form for the year all the charity's funds, incoming resources, revenue expenditure, transfers between funds, all recognised and unrecognised gains and losses on investments, and how the fund balances have changed since the last balance sheet date.

This comprehensive primary accounting statement should show what funds the charity has and how they have been used. Of course, it may be necessary to add appropriate additional information in the notes to the accounts to bring out some special feature, for example, the equipping of a medical research laboratory or the effectiveness of a particular fundraising campaign or significant branch activities.

However, the SOFA is not as radical as it sounds. As we will see, it essentially amalgamated the old-style income and expenditure account with the reconciliation and analysis of the movement of funds.

Reasoning

The SOFA recognises that charities do not usually have a single indicator of performance that is comparable to the bottom line for business. As well as considering the changes in the amounts of the net resources of a charity, it is important to consider the changes in the nature of those resources. As a result, both the SORP and the Regulations recommended a primary statement that records the resources entrusted to a charity and reflects the financial activities thereof.

The SOFA can be divided into two parts: a statement of operations and a statement of other changes in net assets. However, many charities' accounts show that the distinctions based on operations tend to be somewhat arbitrary and are dependent on the impossible task of trying to match a charity's income and expenditure when, as we have seen, in most cases no such match is possible – or even desirable. The SOFA, therefore, moved away from giving undue emphasis to the bottom line based on matching and dropped the use of the words 'surplus' and 'deficit'. It focuses instead on the periodic measurement of the changes in both the nature and amounts of all the net resources of a charity.

Format

A columnar format was scheduled in the 1995 Regulations and reinforced in the 2000 version, (unlike the 1988 SORP 2 where this presentation was merely recommended). The minimum required is one column for unrestricted funds, one for restricted funds, one for endowed funds and one for the total for the year. A fifth column is needed showing the comparative total for the previous, but it is not a legal requirement to have to show comparatives for each type of fund.

However, where there have been no movements in any particular fund, or the charity does not have that type of fund, it is not necessary to include that column. In other words, columns need to be included only where the actual funds exist and there has been movement on them. This columnar approach can be added to: for example, unrestricted funds can be split between general-purpose funds and other unrestricted funds. Whilst, of course, funds may be summarised in this way, if there is more than one restricted fund, details should be shown in the notes to the accounts.

Historically, prior to 1995, many charities either combined all funds and showed what is now the total column, or produced separate income and expenditure accounts for each fund without any total for all funds. Both methods of reporting were effectively ruled out in 1995, as the SOFA must be in the prescribed columnar format.

This format also introduced standard headings for each row (i.e. line), such as incoming resources, charitable resources expended, cost of generating funds, etc., which has helped make charity accounts more comparable. Again, as the SORP makes clear, this information will always be required, but if there has been no movement on a particular heading in the year or previous year, then that heading need not be included.

Functional classification of expenditure means that instead of disclosing expenditure by type (that is, natural classification – cost centre), such as rent, rates, light and heat, salaries, etc., expenditure will be described by its nature, such as charitable expenditure, cost of generating funds, etc. This helps the reader understand what the charity is doing and how much it is spending on these activities.

Additionally, the SOFA includes a statement of gains and losses covering both realised and unrealised gains and losses for investment assets, but only realised gains and losses for tangible assets.

Structure

The SOFA is a single accounting statement whose objective is to show all incoming resources and how those resources have been utilised by the charity in furtherance of its charitable objectives. It should show whether there has been a net inflow or outflow of resources, including capital gains and losses on assets, and provide a reconciliation of all movements in the charity's funds for the year. The incoming resources and resources expended must be analysed clearly and there must be a distinction between unrestricted income funds, restricted income funds and endowment funds. Where a charity has more than one type of fund the SOFA should take a columnar approach and the movements in the different types of funds as well as the total movements of all the funds should be shown. Comparative figures for the previous financial year need be shown only for line totals rather than for each of the columns (see the example below, which is again taken from the author's example provided for CC66 SORP 2000 *Example Reports and Accounts*).

Incoming resources where material should be analysed is as follows:

- Donations, legacies and similar incoming resources (SORP, paragraphs 87–94).
- Incoming resources from operating activities of the charity distinguishing between (SORP, paragraphs 101–8):
  - activities in furtherance of the charity's objects, and
  - activities for generating funds.
- Investment income (SORP, paragraphs 112 and 113).
- Other incoming resources (SORP, paragraph 118).
- The total by column of the resources arising in the year.

The incoming resources need not be shown in the order above and if there is no incoming resource falling into a particular category, then it does not need to be shown at all. As far as resources expended are concerned, again these should be analysed as appropriate to the charity and shown separately where material as follows:

- Cost of generating funds (SORP, paragraphs 132–5).
- Charitable expenditure showing separately:
  - grants payable in furtherance of the charity's objects (SORP, paragraphs 138–46),
  - costs of activities in furtherance of the charity's objects (SORP, paragraphs 147–50),
  - support costs for above where material (SORP, paragraphs 147–50), and
  - resources expended on managing and administering the charity (SORP, paragraphs 151–2).
- The total by column of the above resources expended in the year.

Each column should be totalled to show the net incoming/outgoing resources before transfers. All material transfers between the different classes of funds should then be shown separately and should not be netted off, but be shown gross. Each column will then be totalled to show the net incoming/outgoing resources before revaluations and investment asset disposals. The subsequent section records separately:

- gains and losses on revaluation of fixed assets for the charity's own use; and
- Gains and losses on revaluation and disposal of investment assets (SORP, paragraphs 155–6).

Every column of the SOFA will be totalled to show the net movement in the charity's funds for the year. The net movement in total charity funds should be reconciled to the funds in the balance sheet as follows:

- net movement in funds for the year;
- total funds brought forward;
- total funds carried forward.

In order to comply with FRS3, if a charity has discontinued any of its operations or acquired new ones, the SOFA should distinguish between continuing, discontinued and acquired operations. Normally, this will apply to the whole of a distinctive type of activity of a charity, but not to the development (or cessation) of new projects within that activity.

The SOFA should be prepared following the structure outlined above for all charities. However, individual charities should feel free to expand it wherever necessary in order to present a true and fair view and to give the reader a proper understanding of the nature of all their activities. Clearly, the Charity Commission is recommending that a charity's aim must be to have a clear link between the incoming and outgoing resources and in particular the functional split of activities. Therefore incoming resources and resources expended can be linked together by using similar or identical headings in different parts of the SOFA. Additionally, a charity may find it helpful to have extra columns – for example, to highlight the financial impact of a particular activity.

Indeed, some charities may find it informative to their readers to insert an additional sub-total after the costs of generating funds. Where this is done the sub-total should be called 'net incoming resources available for charitable application' and a further sub-total may be inserted for the total costs of charitable expenditure (see the example below, p. 40). However, whilst the SOFA can be adapted it must be remembered that disclosure requirements must always be met and the underlying structure should not be changed. Therefore, trustees need to balance the provision of information with clarity and remember that the accounts must provide a true and fair view. Any headings should be omitted where there is nothing to report in both the current and preceding financial periods under review. The notes to the accounts should give a description of the sources of any material incoming resources.

Example 5.1

ARTS THEATRE TRUST LIMITED

Consolidated Statement of Financial Activities (including Income and Expenditure Account) for the year ended 31 March 2001

	Note	Un-restricted Funds £'000	Restricted Funds £'000	Total Funds 2001 £'000	Total Funds 2000 £'000
Incoming Resources					
Incoming resources from operation of theatre and arts centre	3	1,200		1,200	1,259
Incoming resources from activities for generating funds	4	549		549	296
Donations		12	79	91	79
Investment income		18	1	19	16
Total incoming resources		1,779	80	1,859	1,650
Less cost of generating funds	4	337	2	339	280
Net incoming resources available for charitable application		1,442	78	1,520	1,370
Charitable expenditure					
Cost of operation of theatre and arts centre	5	1,209	81	1,290	1,230
Managing and administering of the charity	6	150	2	152	113
Total charitable resources expended		1,359	83	1,442	1,343
Net movement in total funds for the year – Net income/ (expenditure)		83	(5)	78	27
Total funds brought forward		1,294	17	1,311	1,284
Total funds carried forward	16+17	1,377	12	1,389	1,311

This statement of financial activities includes all gains and losses recognised in the year. All incoming resources and resources expended derive from continuing activities.

Incoming resources

As the SORP makes clear, all incoming resources becoming available to the charity during the year should be recognised in the statement of financial activities (SOFA). This includes all income belonging to the charity regardless of its source or of the purpose to which it is to be put or has been put (SORP, paragraph 75).

The value of all resources accruing to a charity should be recorded in its SOFA provided it is prudent to so do. The practicality of this needs to be looked at and income should not be recognised until any conditions relating to its receipt have been met. The three factors relevant are entitlement, certainty and measurement. Legal enforceability is essential and charities using the accruals basis should not include income where there is an uncertainty as to their entitlement.

Conditions and restrictions

If a charity receives income which is subject to restrictions, the income should be recorded in the accounts in full, albeit in the restricted fund column. The charity needs to recognise this income as if there has been a transfer of economic benefit from the donor to the charity (SORP, paragraph 85).

This is distinct from incoming resources received subject to certain conditions. Conditions create barriers that must be overcome before the income can be recognised. Timing (such as a three-year grant) is one such example of a condition. In this situation the next two years are a condition to be overcome and this income should therefore be deferred (SORP, paragraph 79). In this case the notes to the accounts should analyse the movement between incoming resources deferred in the year in question and income released in relation to earlier years (SORP, paragraph 83).

Where charities receive funding by way of capital grants to finance the purchase of fixed assets, there was a potential conflict as to how SSAP 4 and the 1995 SORP required the grant to be shown in the accounts. This has now been resolved by the revised SORP, which indicates that funds received for the restricted purpose of providing fixed assets should be accounted for immediately as restricted funds. However, there is no general rule in relation to the treatment of the fixed assets acquired with the funds and this will depend on the basis on which they are held. The fixed asset may be held in a restricted fund or an unrestricted fund dependent upon the terms attached to the gift (SORP, paragraph 86).

Legacies

Put simply, legacy income must be included in the SOFA unless it is incapable of financial measurement. This means that the legacy will have been received, or it is reasonably certain that it will be received and that the value of it can be measured with some degree of reliability. This is certainly one of those cases where the factors of entitlement, certainty and measurement come into play. As an example there will be reasonable certainty and obviously entitlement once the charity has had a letter from, say, the solicitors dealing with an estate advising them that a payment of legacy will be made or that property has been bequeathed and will be transferred.

However, at this stage it may not be possible to measure in financial terms the amount of the legacy and therefore until that can happen it should not be included in the accounts. Once a charity receives a payment on account or a letter advising that such a payment will be made, then this amount should be treated as receivable and included in the accounts. This would be the case even where the letter is received after the end of the financial year, but it is clear that it had been agreed prior to the year-end. It is unlikely in practice that entitlement, certainty of receipt and measurability conditions will be satisfied before the charity has been advised (SORP, paragraphs 89–93).

Assets left to a charity, such as investments, property, etc., should be valued and brought into the accounts at that value. Where the charity has been notified of material legacies which have not been included in the accounts, this fact, and an estimate of the amounts receivable, should be disclosed in the notes to the accounts (SORP, paragraph 94).

Often the charity will be informed that it is the beneficiary of a will some time before probate. At this point it is often difficult to quantify the final amount the charity will eventually receive and so it cannot be included in the accounts for that particular accounting year. If the charity does know the amount it will be in receipt of by the time the accounts are finalised, then an amount should be included in the accounts for this.

The charity will need to include in the accounts an accounting policy
in respect of this. The following is just one example:

> 'Legacies are taken into account when capable of financial
> measurement. In the case of a pecuniary legacy this is on notifi-
> cation, and in all other cases when receivable.'

In circumstances where the charity is entitled to a legacy but has not yet
received the funds, the following example disclosure is made:

> '17 FUTURE LEGACIES
> At 31 August 1997 the Trust was entitled to two legacies
> which had not been received: a legacy expected to yield in the
> region of £12,000 from the late Mr Leonard Cox; and a legacy
> expected to yield in the region of £50,000 from the late
> Mrs Lucy Wakeford.'

Intangible income

A charity may receive assistance in the form of donated facilities, donated
services or beneficial loan arrangements. Such assistance is generally
referred to as 'intangible income'. Such intangible income should be
included in the SOFA only if the charity would otherwise have had to
purchase the donated facilities, the benefit is quantifiable, material and
where the donor is paying the costs involved. An equivalent amount
should be included in the Statement of Financial Activities as expenditure
under the appropriate heading. Details of amounts falling under this
heading should be disclosed in the notes to the accounts (SORP,
paragraphs 99 and 100).

Some charities receive substantial amounts of voluntary help. Such
help should not be accounted for in the Statement of Financial Activities,
but should be dealt with in the notes to the accounts or in the Trustees'
Annual Report. An example of this is ChildLine, which relies on its
volunteer force to answer the telephones. This is often included in the
Trustees Report with a note of thanks.

An example of the ChildLine accounting policy is given below:

> '**Donated assets**
> Donated assets are capitalised at a value equivalent to market value
> at the date of donation.'

Assets are then written off to the SOFA over their useful life via a depreciation charge.

Gifts in kind

The SORP, paragraph 95 states:

> 'Incoming resources in the form of gifts in kind should be included in the Statement of Financial Activities in the following ways:
>
> a Assets given for distribution by the charity should be recognised as incoming resources for the year only when distributed.
>
> b Assets given for use by the charity (e.g. property for its own occupation) should be recognised as incoming resources when receivable.
>
> c Where a gift has been made in kind but on trust for conversion into cash and subsequent application by the charity, the incoming resource should normally be recognised in the accounting period when receivable. However, in certain cases this will not be practicable (e.g. second-hand goods donated for resale in charity shops). In these cases the income should be included in the accounting period in which the gift is sold.'

In all cases the amount at which gifts in kind are brought into account should be either a reasonable estimate of their value to the charity or the amount actually realised. The basis of any valuation should be disclosed. Where material, an adjustment should be made to the original valuation upon subsequent realisation of the gift.

Netting off

All incoming resources, as far as practicable, should be reported gross (SORP, paragraph 76). This means in particular that expenditure on fundraising should not be netted off against the funds raised but should be separately disclosed. The SORP accepts that on occasions this may not be practicable and in these cases the reason for netting off should be given.

Operating activities

The underlying principle in respect of the bringing in of trading figures into the accounts is that netting off of income and expenditure should be kept to a minimum. One area in which this principle may significantly affect charity accounts is the reporting of fundraising income, particularly from shops. In the past, many charities only brought in the net figures. As a result of the 1995 SORP, the income and expenditure in respect of charitable trading such as the sale of donated goods has been shown gross, that is, separately under the appropriate incoming resources and resources expended headings.

However, sales by shops of bought-in goods through trading subsidiaries could be shown net because this was regarded as a non-charitable activity. As most charity shops sell both donated and bought-in goods, this treatment could become very complicated. This position is now changed by the revised SORP.

For the purposes of analysing incoming resources from operating activities such income should be analysed between what is derived from activities in furtherance of the charity's objects and what comes from activities specifically undertaken for generating funds. In the accounts any charity should seek to explain further the activities that it carries out and expand the heading accordingly. Whilst this will probably not be sensible on the face of the SOFA, incoming resources should be shown this way with further information given in the notes to the accounts.

However, all incoming resources received for activities that are in the nature of a payment for the provision of goods or services should be combined under the relevant activity. Thus income from trading and grants or donations that have conditions that make them similar in economic terms to trading income, such as a service agreement with local authorities, should be aggregated. However, grants to fund core activities continue to be regarded as donations and included under the heading 'donations, legacies and similar incoming resources'.

As the SORP itself puts it (paragraph 104) activities in furtherance of the charity's objects may include the sale of goods or services as part of the directly charitable activities of the charity, the letting of non-investment property in furtherance of the objects and the sale of goods or services made or provided by the beneficiaries of the charity. However, activities that are for the purpose of generating funds, which can include selling donated goods, selling bought-in goods, fundraising events such as jumble sales, firework displays, etc., and those sponsorships and social lotteries (which are not donations) are not part of the directly charitable activities. Therefore, these need to be accounted for separately. The following checklist, originally produced by Graham Smith of the Charity Commission and updated in light of the changes to the revised SORP, provides further guidance to charities facing problems in this area. It is cross-referenced to the revised SORP and is a very useful *aide-mémoire*.

		SORP **(paragraph)**
1	If a charity's operating activity is primary purpose trading or ancillary thereto then exempt from income tax and corporation tax under s.505, ICTA 1988.	104
2	If work in connection with trade carried out by beneficiaries or ancillary thereto also exempt from income tax and corporation tax under s.505, ICTA 1988.	104
3	Fees/grants from Government or public authorities for goods/services under one and two above.	104
4	For 1- and 2-type trading carried out by a charity show income/ expenditure gross in SOFA.	104
5	Separate heading required in SOFA for 1–3 above as 'activities' in furtherance of the charity's objects.	104
6	If trade carried out by subsidiary for benefit of charity then the subsidiary must show results using normal accounting rules	110
7	Show separately in SOFA any payments by subsidiary to charity.	107
8	Trading results of subsidiary will only be accounted for by charity in charity's consolidated SOFA of the charity group.	109
9	If trading subsidiary is carrying out primary purpose trading then its reserves should be included in the group balance sheet as 'trading funds' as part of the group's unrestricted charitable funds.	
10	If occasional trading permitted usually fundraising (e.g. jumble sales) then show gross in SOFA under 'activities for generating funds'.	105
11	Sale of donated goods should be shown gross under 'activities for generating funds'.	106
12	For 10 and 11, operating costs should be shown in SOFA 'Costs of generating funds'.	132

Wherever possible the incoming resources and resources expended to each different type of activity should be segregated; indeed, this may have to be done for tax purposes. Charity trustees should consider the balance of the activities being undertaken to determine the most appropriate place to include the incoming resources from such enterprises. One example given in the SORP (paragraph 107) is that of a charity shop that sells mainly donated and bought-in goods, but also sells goods made by the beneficiaries and uses the premises for providing information about the charity. In other words, there is a mix of economic activity. In this case it would be acceptable to class all the incoming resources from the shop under 'activities for generating funds', although there is clearly a mix and some of the income is coming from 'activities in furtherance of the charity's objects'.

It is important that the presentation adopted and the disclosure in the notes are sufficiently detailed to understand the main activities and distinguish the assets and liabilities and transactions of the charity from those of its subsidiary(ies) (SORP, paragraph 108). (For further matters relating to the consolidation of a charity and its subsidiary's accounts see Chapter 10.)

Investment income

Income from investments such as dividends, interest and property rents should be included under the heading 'investment income' in the SOFA. This, however, should not include capital returns, that is to say, capital growth. The notes to the accounts should show this gross investment income analysed between the different types of investment held as laid down in the paragraphs of the SORP dealing with the balance sheet. As a minimum this would be:

- investment properties;
- investments listed on a recognised stock exchange;
- investments in subsidiary or associated undertakings;
- other unlisted securities;
- cash held as part of the investment portfolio;
- any other investments.

Other income

Incoming resources from government and other public authorities can be the result of grants, contracts or service agreements. The SORP recommends that such resources should be treated in a similar manner to other incoming resources and included under the relevant heading in the SOFA.

Thus grants will normally be included under 'donations, legacies and similar incoming resources', whilst payment for contracts/service agreements (that is, fees) would normally be included under 'activities in furtherance of the charity's objects'. Any conditions imposed would obviously need to be taken account of, particularly where these turn the incoming resource into restricted income. Again, the notes to the accounts should give a full description of the sources of any material incoming resources by category (SORP, paragraphs 114–18).

Any income that the charity has not been able to categorise under the specific headings set out in the SORP will be regarded as 'other incoming resources'. In all cases this should be very much in the minority and it is probably true to say that many charities will not need to make any use of this category. As the SORP puts it: 'the most common example is the gain on the disposal of a fixed asset for the charity's own use'.

Cost allocation

The definitions of fundraising and administration costs have been amended from those that appeared in the 1995 SORP and the former has been widened considerably and renamed 'costs of generating funds'. The revised SORP has taken the opportunity also to review where administration and fundraising costs should be shown in the SOFA. Costs will still need to be recorded by their 'natural classification', but are reported by their 'functional classification'.

The regulations and the SORP both point out that those charities whose gross income does not exceed £250,000 will not have to provide a 'functional classification' split of costs. Instead they may choose to use a 'natural classification', for example, salaries, wages, rent, rates, etc. In other words, the preparation of 'functional classification' of costs is mandatory only for those charities whose gross annual income is in excess of £250,000.

Whilst making it clear that it is not practicable to define precisely what should be included under each heading as each charity's circumstances are different, the revised SORP does state that the basis for the allocation should be disclosed in the accounting policies. Items of expenditure which involve more than one 'functional classification' should be allocated on a reasonable and consistent basis to the various 'functional classifications', for example, cost of generating funds/support.

Expenditure incurred on activities falling directly within any one 'functional classification' should not be apportioned to any other 'functional classification' (SORP, paragraph 153).

Cost of generating funds

The revised SORP defines this as those costs actually incurred by a charity (or by their agent) in raising funds from whatever source. This will include costs incurred in getting in donations, legacies, carrying out fundraising activities, investment management costs and similar costs. It may also include the costs associated with raising funds for providing goods and services in the furtherance of the charity's objects, but it should not include any of the costs of carrying out those activities. For example, the cost of applying for a lottery grant, advertising performances of a play put on by a charitable theatre company, the costs of negotiating a contract or advertising for students by a charitable school should all be regarded as a cost of generating funds.

The publicity costs associated with fundraising or raising the profile of the charity should be included under this heading, but it will not include publicity costs incurred in furtherance of the charity's objects.

Where material, the different categories of the costs of generating funds should be shown on the face of the SOFA or in the notes to the accounts. An analysis of the major items of expenditure should be given in the notes to the accounts linked wherever possible to the incoming resource categories reflecting the funds raised (SORP, paragraphs 132–5).

Charitable expenditure

Charitable expenditure will comprise all the costs incurred by the charity in meeting its objectives and should, in the SOFA, be analysed between direct costs, grants payable, support costs and management and administration costs. These costs should also include the depreciation of fixed assets that are used wholly or mainly for charitable activities, including projects. This analysis should be further explained in the notes to the accounts so that the reader can understand how the charity spends its resources on its various activities and, where applicable, if the amount is material, it is further recommended that support costs are shown separately in the SOFA (SORP, paragraphs 136, 137 and 147–50).

Grants payable

In the business world generally, expenditure is usually treated as not being incurred until consideration for the expenditure has passed, in other words until something is received in exchange for the expenditure. However, in the case of grant expenditure relating directly to charitable activity, no exchange is involved and this creates problems since it is not possible to match the expenditure with the receipt of goods or services, as there are none.

The revised SORP explains that a grant is a payment made by a charity to an institution or an individual to further the objects of the charity. Grants can be repayable to the charity in certain circumstances (SORP, paragraph 138). There is, therefore, an obligation created by agreeing to make a grant.

Not all obligations are legally binding, particularly where there are conditions involving future and uncertain events and there are uncertainties about passing and receiving the economic benefit promised. As an example, the Cancer Research Campaign, in promising to support a three-year project grant, states that future payments are conditional on availability of funds and on progress results of reviews of the work to be carried out (see further Chapter 6).

Disclosure of grants payable

There was considerable debate about the disclosure of grants payable in a charity's accounts. The revised SORP (SORP, paragraphs 139–46) reached a very sensible compromise on this issue. In SORP, paragraph 140 recommends that if explanation of the grants is needed, then the analysis may be shown in the notes to the accounts, as part of the Trustees' Report or by means of a separate publication.

Whilst information on grants payable should and must be available to anyone who requires it, there is no need to clog up the annual accounts with this information, provided the information is readily available in some other format. Many charities do already provide this information in a separate published document – the Cancer Research Campaign does so in their annual scientific handbook. As SORP, paragraph 139 points out, additional disclosure will not be applicable where the total grant expenditure made by a charity does not exceed 5 per cent of the total expenditure of that charity. In such a case none of the grants will be regarded as material.

The SORP makes clear that the analysis need not cover grants to individuals but must cover those to institutions in detail. Thus for both individual and institutional grants analysis should be given that discloses the total number and the total value of the grants given for different charitable purposes (SORP, paragraph 142). Additionally, for institutional grants, the trustees are required to provide more detail in order to convey a proper understanding of the charity's grant-making activities. Effectively in all cases grants to any one institution in any one accounting year where the total value is at least 2 per cent of total institutional grants in that year should be disclosed although there is no requirement to disclose any grants which are below £1,000 in total. Otherwise the number of grants shown should cover at least the 50 largest institutional grants (SORP, paragraph 143).

Support costs

The Glossary definition is:

> '"Support costs" of charitable activities comprise costs incurred directly in support of expenditure on the objects of the charity, and can therefore be considered as part of total expenditure directly relating to the objects of the charity. Such costs will include all services (either at headquarters or through a regional network) which are identifiable as wholly or mainly in support of the charity's project work or other charitable expenditure (excluding management and administration costs) if – but only if – they are an integral part of the cost of carrying out the direct charitable objectives of the charity.'

The Cancer Research Campaign's objective is the furtherance of research into the causes of cancer. To achieve this objective it makes grants to universities, institutes, hospitals, etc. where research is being carried out. It has at its headquarters a scientific department whose activities, whilst not engaged directly in research, are to assist those who are carrying out the research. Costs of this activity would, therefore, be correctly allocated to support costs.

Management and administration costs

Nothing excites the media more than charities overspending on so-called 'overheads'. Although most of the costs of running a charity can be identified as belonging to either cost of generating funds or support costs, there will always remain costs that are incurred in connection with the management of the charity's assets. These are organisational as opposed to project administration costs and include compliance with constitutional and statutory requirements. Further examples of these costs are:

1 expenditure on trustees, management and annual general meetings;
2 compliance with constitutional and statutory requirements, for example:
  a annual audit fee,
  b most legal fees,
  c valuation fees;
3 management of the charity's assets;
4 organisational management.

Unlike the 1995 SORP, these costs will now be shown as part of the charitable expenditure. However, there should continue to be a clear analysis of all the main items of expenditure on management and administration in the notes to the accounts (SORP, paragraph 152).

Gains and losses on fixed assets

Gains and losses can arise either as realised (e.g. on disposal) or as unrealised (e.g. revaluation or impairment). These gains or losses on fixed asset, whether the asset was held for the charity's own use or for investment purposes, will form part of the particular fund in which the asset concerned is or was held at the time the loss or gain materialised whether realised or unrealised. As the SORP, paragraph 156 puts it:

'Such gains and losses should be recognised as follows:

a Impairment losses of assets held for the charity's own use (i.e. not investments) should be regarded as additional depreciation of the impaired asset and included appropriately in the resources expended section of the Statement of Financial Activities.

b Gains on the disposal of fixed assets for the charity's own use should be included under the heading 'other incoming resources'. Losses on disposal should be treated as additional depreciation and included appropriately in the resources expended section of the Statement of Financial Activities.

c Revaluation gains or losses (which are not considered to be impairment losses (see paragraphs 224–230)) on assets held for the charity's own use should be included in the section on gains and losses on revaluations of fixed assets for the charity's own use.

d Any gains and losses on investment assets (including property investments) should be included under the gains and losses on the revaluation and disposal of investment assets. Realised and unrealised gains and losses may be included in a single line.'

The last sentence of (d) is probably one of the most important changes in the revised SORP.

Branches

The revised SORP has considerably less to say about branches than the 1995 version did. However, it does make it clear that all branch transactions should be accounted for gross in the reporting charity's own accounts, although transactions which net off – for example, branch-to-branch transactions or those between the branches and the head office – may be excluded. Similarly, all assets and liabilities of the branch should be incorporated into the reporting charity's own balance sheet. Thus, for example, funds that have been raised by the branch but not passed on to the reporting charity need to be included as debtors in the same way that cash transferred from the reporting charity to the branch for spending needs to be included as cash at bank by the reporting charity. As ever, throughout the revised SORP materiality is important and transactions and balances which are not material in aggregate do not need to be reported.

Where a branch is not a separate legal entity its accounts must form part of the accounts of the reporting charity, but it can if it wishes produce additional accounts covering only the branch if this is deemed to be in the interest of local supporters and beneficiaries. As far as fund accounting is concerned, the same rules apply to branches as to the reporting charity. That is to say, funds raised for general purposes will be unrestricted and those raised by a branch for specific purposes will be restricted.

6   Balance Sheet

Introduction

The balance sheet needs to show the state of affairs at the end of the financial year (SORP, paragraphs 181–271).

The 1995 Charities SORP did not introduce many changes to the balance sheet, although the changes to the recognition of income and expenditure and fund accounting, for some charities, had a considerable effect on the size of the figures that had to be included. For instance, the writing back of deferred, restricted income included originally under creditors and treated as a restricted fund carried forward greatly strengthens the balance sheet.

There had been many arguments about what a balance sheet is supposed to represent. As long ago as April 1993 the Accounting Standards Board (ASB) produced a discussion paper on 'the role of valuation in financial reporting'. There was a problem in UK accounting in that there was no consistency in valuation practice. This particularly affected the valuation of assets, which may appear in the balance sheet at current revaluation, a previous revaluation or original historic cost. The ASB saw this as unsatisfactory and suggested that a prescriptive approach should be followed, using one of three options.

The 1995 SORP moved well ahead of that debate and provided considerable guidance on balance sheet valuation, although it still accepted generally accounted principles, as does the 2000 version. It is perhaps worth bearing in mind that although the only significant reference in the 1995 regulations to the SORP occurred in relation to the valuation of assets and liabilities, there are considerably more references in the 2000 version – see in particular the Schedule to Regulation 3 (10) dealing with notes to the accounts 1. (k), (l), (m), (q), (s), (t) and (u).

Presentation

The funds of a charity should be grouped together in the balance sheet according to type, distinguishing between endowments, other restricted funds, designated and other unrestricted funds as the SORP explains. Further analysis of major individual funds needs to be given, as appropriate, in the notes to the accounts.

The assets of the charity should be analysed in the balance sheet between fixed, including those for charity use and those for investment, and current assets, whilst liabilities should be analysed between current and long-term elements, with the total (if material) of any provisions for liabilities or charges shown separately. The totals for both short-term and long-term creditors should be sub-analysed in the notes.

In addition, the assets and liabilities should be analysed in a way that enables the reader to gain a proper appreciation of their spread and character. The balance sheet must be approved by all the trustees as a body, but need be signed by only one of them on behalf of all. It must, of course always be dated.

Investments

The recommendation in the 1995 SORP that long-term investments, including property, should be included at market value in charity accounts, proved to be one of the most controversial of the proposals.

Fixed assets

The treatment of investment assets has been amended in the revised SORP, paragraph 231 to read:

'Investment assets (including investment and investment properties (Appendix 1 Glossary) and cash held for investment) should be classified as a separate category within fixed assets, except where the intention is to realise the asset without reinvestment of the sale proceeds. In such a case it should be reclassified as a current asset. The reason for this is that investment assets are generally held with the overall intention of retaining them long-term (i.e. as fixed assets) for the continuing benefit of the charity in the form of income and capital appreciation.'

Valuation

The revised SORP continues to recommend that all fixed asset investments be valued at market value at the balance sheet date, or at 'the trustees' best estimate of market value'. This is entirely consistent with current commercial accounting practice where directors can estimate the value of investments in periods between obtaining a regular professional valuation (SORP, paragraph 232). For assets other than shares the SORP recommends a 'reasonable approach', which it considers to be to obtain valuations from appropriately experienced persons (such as qualified valuers) at least once every five years (SORP, paragraphs 233 and 234).

Current asset position

Investments that do not fall within the definition of fixed asset investments will be current assets and be valued at the lower of cost and net realisable value. The decision to classify certain investments as current assets will be partially determined by trustee intentions.

Analysis

The SORP, paragraph 238 states that in the notes to the accounts an analysis of investment assets should be provided such as property, 'stocks and shares' both listed and unlisted, cash and any other investments. A basic minimum is prescribed and the SORP also suggests that there should be a geographical split (i.e. UK and outside), together with details of a heavy concentration in any one investment (in excess of 5 per cent of the portfolio) and any material restrictions which might apply on the realisation of any such assets (SORP, paragraphs 239–40). Where investments are held within more than one of the charity's funds, a distinction should be made as to which fund the investment belongs.

Gains and losses

The inclusion of investments at market value means that charities are making unrealised as well as realised gains and losses. The unrealised gain/loss to be included in the separate section of the statement of financial activities will be the difference between the market value at the closing balance sheet date and the market value at the opening balance sheet date or the cost price if the investment asset was acquired during the year. Any gains and losses on investment assets (including property investments) should be included under the gains and losses on the revaluation and disposal of investment assets. Realised and unrealised gains and losses may be included in a single line (see further Chapter 5).

Example 6.1

ARTS THEATRE TRUST LIMITED

Consolidated and Charity Balance Sheets as at 31 March 2001

	Note	Group 2001 £'000	Group 2000 £'000	Charity 2001 £'000	Charity 2000 £'000
Fixed Assets					
Tangible assets	10	830	824	830	824
Investments	4	–	–	1	1
		830	824	831	825
Current Assets					
Stocks	11	217	213	203	212
Debtors	12	207	206	272	206
Cash at bank and in hand		423	319	314	319
		847	738	789	737
Creditors: amounts falling due within one year	13	242	195	185	195
Net Current Assets		605	543	604	542
Total assets less current liabilities		1,435	1,367	1,435	1,367
Creditors: amounts falling due after more than one year	15	46	56	46	56
		1,389	1,311	1,389	1,311
Funds					
Unrestricted funds					
General	16	1,210	1,263	1,210	1,263
Designated	16	167	31	167	31
		1,377	1,294	1,377	1,294
Restricted funds	17	12	17	12	17
		1,389	1,311	1,389	1,311

Approved by the board on 13 June 2001 and signed on its behalf by

....

S.A. Bloggs, Chairman

The treatment of liabilities

Under normal circumstances there needs to be an exchange of goods or services for expenditure to be recognised in the accounts. However, grant-making charities, and the application of direct charitable expenditure for other charities, poses potential difficulties in applying this principle. The reason is that there is often no tangible exchange for the consideration given.

SORP treatment

The revised SORP makes the point that a liability is an obligation to transfer economic benefit. Therefore, it considers that it results from a duty or responsibility that places a legal or constructive obligation on the charity to make a payment then, or at some time in the future. However, a moral obligation, such as results from the making of a non-contractual promise, does not create a liability unless it meets the definition set out in the SORP (Appendix 1.19).

Practical implementations

If a charity wishes to make a £30,000 grant over three years, for example, how much should be charged in the first year's accounts? Many charities would seek to charge the full £30,000, citing prudence as part of their reasoning. The SORP states that in this situation the charge to the SOFA for the grant payable should be on the basis of how the expenditure has been incurred or was due to be incurred. In other words has a liability arisen? (See further pp. 50 and 59).

Commitments

The revised SORP makes a distinction between those commitments of a binding nature and those that are a mere 'intention'. FRS12, which deals with provisions, contingent liabilities and contingent assets, is generally applicable to charities (SORP, paragraphs 119–30 and 250–64). Binding commitments (that is, where there is a legal or constructive obligation, in accordance with FRS12) should be accounted for as stated above (SORP, paragraph 250). The amount to be recognised as the liability should be the charity's best estimate of the expenditure required to settle the obligation at the balance sheet date (SORP, paragraph 251). Where provisions are accrued but are to be paid over several years, future payments may have a reduced value and. if the effect is material, the figures should be discounted (SORP, paragraph 252). In all cases the best estimate of the liability should be reviewed at the balance sheet date and adjusted appropriately (SORP, paragraph 253).

Where the trustees' promise cannot be legally enforced, the trustees may set up a designated reserve to cover possible future intentions. This is only where the expenditure is to be incurred out of existing unrestricted funds. If, however, the 'intention' is to be funded from future income, for accounting purposes it should be ignored (SORP, paragraph 255).

The notes to the accounts should show the particulars of all material provisions for commitments, which have been accrued in the balance sheet as liabilities. These particulars should show the amounts involved, when the commitments are likely to be met and the movements on commitments previously reported. The notes to the accounts should set out in detail the commitments included on the balance sheet as liabilities and differentiate from those that are intentions to spend and not included on the balance sheet. All designated funds should be separately disclosed as part of the unrestricted funds of the charity in the notes to the accounts (SORP, paragraphs 256–9).

Contingent liabilities

This sub-section of the revised SORP, which also deals with contingent assets, has been specifically cross-referenced to FRS12. There are yet more references to the use of the notes to the accounts than occurred in the 1995 SORP. In particular, details of material items are called for in SORP paragraph 266, while SORP, paragraph 267 recommends that disclosure of the full details of the nature of the contingency.

Disclosure is required not just of the assets subject to mortgage or charge but in addition the charity will need to provide 'particulars' of them (SORP, paragraph 270). However, it will not be necessary to list out 'amounts and interest and repayment terms for all loan liabilities'. It will be necessary to disclose as a separate item in the accounts 'the interest payable' as well as 'loans made to subsidiaries, security provided and repayment terms' (SORP, paragraph 271).

In summary

The revised SORP provides a more consistent treatment for the correct recognition of liabilities, that is, only accounting for expenditure which has or was to be incurred in the year. The question of when a charity recognises a liability and how it reports it as expenditure can now be answered with more conviction. In all cases it is important to consider each grant and other direct charitable expenditure on an individual basis. It is certainly true to say that not all liabilities have legal obligations. FRS 5, which is equally applicable to charities as to other entities, recognises that entities may be commercially or morally liable for the enforcement of a contract. The trustees may deem their intention to be 'binding' and hence the transaction should be accounted for in this year's accounts.

Some FRS effects

This section looks particularly at some of those FRSs, not dealt with earlier, which have come into force since the 1995 SORP and which affect charity accounting in respect of the balance sheet.

FRS 10 – Goodwill and intangible assets

FRS 10 requires that any goodwill purchased, as well as intangible fixed assets, where those have a market value, should be capitalised on the balance sheet and written off over their life, which is usually expected to be twenty years, subject to any impairment review (see further 6.5.2 FRS 11). Whilst it is unlikely that many charities will have any goodwill purchased since charities are not in the habit of acquiring going concerns, many may have intangible assets. In this case if the charity has an intangible asset that does not meet the criteria set out in FRS 10 it should not be included in the accounts, but details of the asset and any financial effect must be disclosed in the notes to the accounts (SORP, paragraph 189).

FRS 11 – Impairment of tangible fixed assets

FRS 11 sets out the principles and methodology for accounting for impairment of fixed assets and goodwill. The carrying amount of an asset is compared with its recoverable amount and if the carrying amount is higher then the asset is written down. Recoverable amount is defined as the higher of the amount that could be obtained by selling the asset (net realisable value) and the amount that could be obtained through using the asset (value in use). Impairment tests are only required where there has been some indication that an impairment has occurred (SORP, paragraphs 224–30).

It is unlikely, and in fact rare, for a functional asset to become impaired. This will occur if its net book value is higher than the amount that could be recovered if the asset was disposed of. In any case like this FRS 11 would have the effect of requiring the asset to be written down to the recoverable amount. As the SORP, paragraph 226, puts it, impairment is indicated by:

'a physical deterioration, change or obsolescence of the fixed asset;

b social (demographic or environmental) changes resulting in a reduction of beneficiaries for a charity;

c changes in the law, other regulations or standards which adversely affect the activities of a charity;

d management commitments to undertake a significant reorganisation;

e a major loss of key employees associated with particular activities of a charity;

f operating losses on activities using fixed assets primarily to generate incoming resources.'

In these cases the charity should first determine what the net realisable value of the asset is. If this is lower than the net book value, the charity will need to consider the value in use. If the value in use is considered to be above the net book value, the asset should be valued at the net book value; if however it is below, impairment has occurred. In this case the impairment loss needs to be recognised in accordance with the requirements of FRS 11 and the loss should be treated as additional depreciation and included in the SOFA in accordance with paragraph 198 of the SORP. In these cases the methods used in the impairment test to determine the net realisable value and the value in use should be disclosed in the notes to the accounts.

FRS 15 – tangible fixed assets

The main effects of FRS 15 are as follows:

- All fixed assets should be included in the charity's balance sheet.

- If a charity carries fixed assets at valuation then this valuation must be kept up to date.
- Depreciation is a measure of use of wearing out of an asset and is therefore nearly always required.
- Expenditure incurred on looking after a fixed asset does not obviate the need for depreciation; instead the economic life of the asset should be reconsidered in the light of the expenditure.

This somewhat bald summary camouflages the nuances incorporated in the FRS and also in the revised SORP. However, there is a danger of assuming that because the revised SORP has several pages devoted to this issue, and also because the FRS itself specifically refers to charities, charities are accorded special treatment under the FRS and it can therefore be ignored. This is not the case. The revised SORP supports the view that all fixed assets should be included in the balance sheet except for certain historic and/or inalienable assets.

Examples are provided in the revised SORP of the sort of asset in question (SORP, paragraph 208); however, the key distinction is between assets that are retained as a means by which the charity achieves its objects and those which exist purely as part of its objects. A war memorial, for example, is the chief object of a war memorial preservation society and is therefore of no value in the accounts as it represents the very rationale of the charity. No distinction is drawn between donated and purchased assets on the balance sheet.

Neither FRS 15 nor the revised SORP requires charities to carry fixed assets at valuation, apart from investments. Even if an asset has already been carried at valuation before the FRS was effective (23 March 2000) there is no need for assets to be revalued regularly. This balance sheet value is the initial carrying amount and is treated as if it were cost and the assets held at cost, instead of valuation, are not subject to the requirement to revalue regularly, although they do still require an impairment review if appropriate. However, note that subsequently the FRS will require assets that have been revalued to be revalued formally every five years, with interim valuations every three years, and further reviews each year if there is evidence of a material change in value.

Thus assets that are capitalised sometime after being acquired – for example, as a result of a change in accounting policy – should be included at original cost or at the value at which the gift was included in the SOFA less an amount for depreciation. However, if neither of these amounts is ascertainable a reasonable estimate of the asset's cost or current value to the charity should be used. Such a valuation will be regarded as the asset's initial carrying amount and will not be regarded as a revaluation (SORP, paragraph 195). For the vast majority of charities, the valuation issue will be of material significance only when considering property. The FRS sets out various types of valuation approach, clearly pointing to those that are the most suitable for charities:

- non-specialised properties – existing use basis;
- specialised properties – depreciated replacement cost;
- surplus properties – open market values;
- other fixed assets – open market value or depreciated replacement cost.

FRS 15 requires valuations to be done by qualified external experts, or internally as long as the valuation is subject to an external review. However, it also recognises that there will be limited cost benefits to charities in this valuation process and therefore permits charities to adopt other reasonable approaches to arrive at a valuation. This does not mean that charities can avoid the valuation issue altogether; rather, that they can avoid the expense and time involved in the more formal approach suggested by FRS 15. The revised SORP picks up this point by permitting some flexibility in this area by allowing the trustees to exercise more of their own judgement in obtaining an appropriate valuation.

The FRS specifically addresses the position of charities in two other areas, again both mirrored in the revised SORP. First, it acknowledges that donated assets can be treated as received at cost rather than revaluation (SORP, paragraph 194); and second, it relaxes the valuation requirements on inalienable and historic assets (SORP, paragraphs 208–17). The FRS and the revised SORP also permit charities to use indices where appropriate. This is certainly a welcome relief from the detailed requirement of more formal valuations. Where an index is used, it will need to be adjusted every year.

Following intense lobbying by heritage organisations, the Charity Commission has signalled that it will allow them to rely in most circumstances on the exemption granted by FRS 15 where the information benefit of including these assets on the balance sheet would be outweighed by the cost of establishing a sensible value. Newly acquired assets, however, will commonly have an obvious value, and these will have to be included on the balance sheet. Therefore, there will usually be no need to capitalise inalienable and historic fixed assets that are already held.

Turning now to depreciation and expenditure incurred on looking after a fixed asset, these are much more straightforward. FRS 15 requires all tangible fixed assets to be depreciated over their useful life. It is no longer appropriate to rely on the phrase that the charity maintains its assets/properties in good order and that therefore no depreciation is necessary. Where such expenditure is incurred, it prolongs the useful life of the asset and so may affect the depreciation, but this does not remove entirely the need for depreciation. Freehold land is still excluded, as are assets where any depreciation would be immaterial either because the residual value is so high on eventual disposal or because the asset has a useful life of over fifty years.

Checklist

1   Are the assets of the charity sub-divided between fixed assets and current assets?
2   Have the fixed assets been subdivided into:
    a intangible assets?
    b tangible assets for the charity's use?
    c inalienable and historic assets?
    d investments?
3   Have fixed assets been divided between those used in direct furtherance of the charity's objects and those used for some other purposes such as the generation of income?
4   Have current assets been divided into:
    a stocks and work in progress?
    b debtors?
    c investments?
    d cash at bank and in hand?
5   Are the liabilities divided between current and long-term liabilities?
6   Is there a heading for net current assets or liabilities?
7   Have the assets and liabilities been analysed in a way that enables a proper appreciation of their spread and character?
8   Is there a heading for total assets less current liabilities?
9   Is there a heading for provisions for liabilities and charges?
10 Has the figure for net assets been given?
11 Have the charity's funds been divided into:

unrestricted income funds?
income funds which are restricted as to their use?
endowment funds?

12   Where the use of any income is time conditional, has it been disclosed as 'deferred income' on the balance sheet, with suitable explanation in the notes?

13   For assets for which there is no readily identifiable market price has a reasonable approach to valuation/revaluation been adopted?

14   Have revaluation increases to assets acquired for charity use been added to the appropriate fixed asset account where applicable?

15   Where there has been a permanent diminution in the value of a fixed asset, has this been appropriately recognised?

16   Have liabilities been correctly identified and recognised, differentiating between amounts payable within the next year and amounts payable after more than one year?

17   Where there is an asset related to the liability has this been shown?

18   Has the balance sheet been approved by the trustees, as a body, and signed by one of them on their behalf?

19   Has the date of approval been stated?

7   Cash Flow Statement

Introduction

Some charities may require a cash flow statement in order to conform
with statements of standard accounting practice and financial reporting
standards. In accordance with SSAP 10, 'statements of source and application of funds', the 1988 SORP 2 recommended that charities should
prepare a source and application of funds statement. SSAP 10 had at this
stage already suffered from many criticisms but, although it was twice
considered for revision, no changes were made.

    Developments internationally requiring the preparation of cash flow
statements led the Accounting Standards Committee to issue in July 1990
an exposure draft which subsequently became the first financial reporting
standard, published by the Accounting Standards Board in 1991. This is
FRS 1 'Cash flow statements'. As the cash flow statement is considered to
be a primary statement, it should be accorded the same prominence in the
accounts as the SOFA and the balance sheet.

FRS 1 (revised 1996)

On 31 October 1996 the Accounting Standards Board published a revised
version of FRS 1, the accounting standard on cash flow statements. This
revision replaced the original FRS 1, issued in September 1991, and
follows on from FRED 10, published in 1995, which detailed the proposed
changes. The new standard applied to company accounting periods
ending on or after 23 March 1997, although earlier use was encouraged.

    FRS 1 requires a genuine cash flow statement, the concept of 'cash
equivalents' having been omitted. There is a definition of cash, to include
cash in hand, deposits and overdrafts repayable on demand. The FRS has
a section dealing with the management of liquid resources which
includes, for example, cash flows relating to short-term deposits and
other items previously regarded as cash equivalents.

    The order and headings for cash flows were restructured and the
reconciliation between the cash flow statement and the balance sheet was

altered to focus on the effect of cash flow on net debt (borrowings less cash and liquid resources). Under certain strict conditions cash inflows and outflows can now be netted off.

The requirement to produce a cash flow statement is dependent on the size of the charity, that is there is a need to refer to FRS 1 (SORP, paragraphs 272–6). Attention should also be paid to the governing instrument of the charity as this may require a cash flow statement.

Threshold

Currently a cash flow statement should be prepared if in either its present or its previous financial year two or more of the following size qualifications are/were met:

- gross income in the year in excess of £2.8 million;
- balance sheet total in excess of £1.4 million;
- More than fifty employees.

Special provisions apply to small groups and in cases where a charity is within the size qualification in some years but not in others. The figures may alter from time to time (Companies Act 1985, ss. 246–9).

SORP

The major difference between FRS 1 and the revised SORP is that whilst the cash flow should comply with the requirement of FRS 1 it will not include movements in endowments from 'operating activities' as these should be treated as increases or decreases in the financing section.

Cash donations to endowments should be treated as additions to endowments, the receipts and payments from the acquisition and disposal of investments should be shown gross in the 'capital expenditure and financial investment' section of the cash flow statement, the very rare payments made out of permanent endowments should be shown as a decrease in the 'financing' section and transactions which do not result in cash flows should not be reported in the cash flow statement (SORP, paragraph 275).

The disclosure requirements of FRS 1 (revised 1996) are dependent upon the way in which the cash flow statement has been prepared and its contents but as the revised SORP, paragraph 275 puts it, it will be necessary to disclose:

'a major transactions not resulting in cash movements should be disclosed in the notes if necessary for an understanding of the underlying transactions – for instance, the release of expendable endowment;

b cash and any financing (movements) should be reconciled to the appropriate opening and closing balance sheet amounts; and

c a reconciliation of cash-flows from 'operating activities' with the cash flow statement to the net incoming resources/expenditure line of the Statement of Financial Activities.'

Exemptions

Charities, whether or not incorporated under the Companies Act, are exempt from FRS 1 if they satisfy the small company limits for the purposes of filing abbreviated accounts with the Registrar of Companies at Companies House. However, attention should be drawn to the reasons for excluding a cash flow statement from their accounts, with the reasons set out in the notes to the accounts.

Homeless International does just this and draws the reader's attention, in its accounting policies, to the fact that a cash flow statement has not been prepared on these grounds. Many other charities also take advantage of the exemption without providing the reasons why, although in most cases these will be obvious. In the booklet produced by the Charity Commission (CC66) *SORP 2000: Example Reports and Accounts,* a number of the examples do not have a cash flow statement and in most cases no reason is shown as to why this has been omitted. To quote:

'One of the cash flow statements (example 5) shows the treatment of donations to a permanent endowment. It also shows the treatment of cash movements in investments assets which form part of an endowment fund (SORP 2000, paragraph 275). Examples 6 and 7 demonstrate that sometimes the cash flow from investment income can be considered as arising from operating activities and sometimes as a return on investments.'

The following example is taken from CC66 and is for a charitable company with one non-charitable subsidiary which has produced consolidated accounts. In the cash flow statement, cash flow from investment income is considered to be part of the 'operational activities' rather than a return on investments as this particular charity considers its investments to be an integral part of its operations. Also included in the example is an extract from the notes to the accounts which supports the cash flow statement.

Example 7.1

THE ABC CHARITY

Consolidated cash flow statement for the year ended 31 March 2001

	Notes	2001 £'000	2000 £'000
Net cash inflow from operating activities	20	2,090	595
Capital expenditure and financial investment			
Payments to acquired tangible fixed assets		(1,990)	(1,000)
Proceeds from sale of tangible fixed assets		130	170
Purchase of investments		(1,200)	(865)
Proceeds from sale of investments		2,300	915
		(760)	(780)
Cash inflow/(outflow) before increase in liquid Resources and financing	20	1,330	(185)
Financing			
Finance lease payments		(40)	(40)
Management of liquid resources			
Increase in short term deposits		(400)	(200)
Increase/(decrease) in cash in the year	20	890	(425)

Statement of changes in resources applied for fixed assets
For charity use for the year ended 31 March 2000

	Unrestricted Funds £'000	Restricted Funds £'000	Totals 2001 £'000	Totals 2000 £'000
Net movement in funds for the year	3,065	(810)	2,255	400
Resources used for net acquisitions of tangible fixed assets	(1,100)	(400)	(1,500)	(590)
Net movement in funds available for future activities	1,965	(1,210)	755	(190)

THE ABC CHARITY

Cash flow information for the group

(a) **Reconciliation of changes in resources to net inflow from operating activities**

	2000 £'000	2001 £'000
Net incoming resources before revaluations	2,155	155
Gain on sale of tangible fixed assets	(20)	(30)
Depreciation	380	270
Decrease in stocks	100	450
Increase in debtors	(765)	(225)
Increase/(decrease) in creditors	240	(20)
Net cash inflow from operating activities	2,090	595

(b) **Reconciliation of net cash flow to movement in net funds/debt**

	2000	2001
Increase/(decrease) in cash in the period	890	(425)
Cash outflow from decrease in lease financing	40	40
Cash outflow from increase in liquid resources	400	200
Movement in net funds and debt in the year	1,330	(185)
Net funds and debt at 1 April 2000	3,020	3,205
Net funds and debt at 31 March 2001	4,350	3,020

(c) **Analysis of net funds/debt**

	1 April 2000 £'000	Cash flow £'000	31 March 2001 £'000
Cash at bank and in hand	200	890	1,090
Liquid resources	3,000	400	3,400
Finance leases	(180)	40	(140)
	3,020	1,330	4,350

8   Disclosure of Accounting Policies and Notes to the Accounts

Introduction

The approach taken in both the regulations and the SORP that the accounts should include an explanation of the accounting policies used to prepare them follows very closely the requirements of both the Companies Act 1985 and FRS 18. FRS 18, which was published after the revised SORP was issued in October 2000, replaces FRED 21, referred to in the SORP, which itself replaced SSAP 2, 'Disclosure of Accounting Policies'. However, and perhaps more importantly, the regulations and the SORP recognise the difficulty that many have in understanding charity accounts. It is clear that the statement of accounting policies must be the most appropriate to give a true and fair view and be detailed enough to cover all material items (SORP, paragraph 277). As the SORP, paragraph 278 puts it:

> 'Accounting policies are the principles, bases, conventions and rules by which transactions are recognised, measured and presented in the accounts. They are supplemented by estimation techniques where judgement is required in recording the value of incoming and outgoing resources and of assets and liabilities. It is essential that the accounts are accompanied by an explanation of the basis and estimation techniques on which they have been prepared. Accounts are normally prepared on the basis that the charity is a going concern and must include relevant, reliable, comparable and under- standable information.'

Accounting standards

True and fair view accounts should follow the standards laid down in SSAPs and FRSs, which have been issued or adopted by the Accounting Standards Board. Any departures must be justified with a full expla- nation, otherwise it may be deemed not to be true and fair (SORP, paragraphs 279–81).

FRS 18 – Disclosure of accounting policies

FRS 18, which replaced SSAP2, promotes the adoption and review of accounting policies most appropriate to the particular circumstances of an organisation for the purpose of giving a true and fair view and of sufficient disclosure for users to understand the policies adopted and how they have been applied. It distinguishes between accounting policies, which are the principles on which the accounts are prepared, and the estimation techniques that an organisation may choose to use in order to provide a monetary value for an asset, liability, gain or loss, in accordance with the adoptive principles in the chosen accounting policies. As Appendix 2 to the SORP puts it, FRS 18 (FRED 21/SSAP 2) is:

> 'Equally applicable to charities as to other organisations but charities preparing receipts and payments accounts (see paragraphs 350 to 356) need only apply the objective of comparability usually by applying consistent policies.'

This part of Appendix 2 (SORP, p. 76 – dealing with SSAP2) defines for the purpose of preparing charity accounts, both the 'going concern' assumption and the 'accruals' concept. It also introduces and seeks to explain the terms referred to earlier: relevance, reliability, comparability and comprensibility.

Accounting policies

Examples of matters on which the accounting policies should be explained where the amounts involved are material include:

- donations;
- grants payable and receivable;
- costs of generating funds;
- charitable expenditure, support costs and costs of management and administration;
- investment assets;
- valuation, capitalisation and depreciation of fixed assets;
- netted off expenses;
- commitments not yet met;
- use of designated funds.

The checklist that follows, whilst not exhaustive, gives some idea of what should be included in accounting policies.

	SORP (paragraph)
(NB: *The statement of accounting policies must cover all material items.*)	
Have the accounts been prepared in accordance with the going concern concept?	Para. 278
Is there a statement as to whether or not the accounts have been prepared in accordance with the charities SORP, applicable FRSs, SSAPs, other SORPs, etc.?	Paras 277 and 279
(NB: *Not obligatory for unincorporated charities with a gross income of less than £100,000 per annum.*)	
Have the accounting policies adopted for dealing with material items and changes been disclosed?	Para. 282
Do the accounting policies stated include specific mention of the following in respect of material items?	
A description of when a legacy is regarded as receivable?	Para. 283(a)
Grants payable?	Para. 284(b)
The basis of allocation of direct charitable expenditure, support costs, cost of generating funds and the cost of management and administration of the charity?	Para. 284(c)
Cost of generating funds?	Para. 284(b)
Investment assets (including investment properties) and the income arising therefrom?	Para. 286
Realised and unrealised gains and losses on investment assets and fixed assets for charity use?	Para. 287
Valuation (if applicable), capitalisation and depreciation of fixed assets for charity use?	Para. 285
Netted off expenses and related income?	Para. 283(g)
Subscriptions for life membership?	Para. 283(e)
Stocks of unsold or unused goods and materials?	Para. 288
The use of designated funds?	Para. 290

Have the balance sheet values of all assets and
liabilities been calculated in accordance with
the methods and principles in the SORP and
included at the following amounts:
Fixed assets for the charity's use, at cost less
   depreciation?   Para. 285
Investments, whether classified as fixed or
   current assets, at market value?   Para. 286
Liabilities at settlement value?   Para. 284(a)
Is all expenditure on the acquisition,
enhancement, production or installation of
fixed assets for the charity's use capitalised
other than where the asset is inalienable or
historic?   Para. 285
Are fixed assets held for charity's use, with
finite useful lives, suitably depreciated and
charged against charitable expenditure, as
appropriate?   Para. 285
Has the basis for measuring material gifts in kind
been disclosed?   Para. 283(b)
Have trustees established the legal status of
different parts of their organisation
(e.g. branches)?   Para. 281
Have any material departures from accounting
standards been stated?   Para. 280

This is probably the most comprehensive part of the SORP and this revised
version has taken the opportunity to group together all of its accounting
policy notes in one clearly defined section (SORP, paragraphs 277–91).

Notes

Whilst 'notes to the accounts' are covered in considerable detail in a
schedule to the regulations, this is not so in the case of the SORP.
Comments on general accounting notes remain scattered throughout the
text. The matter of what to include in the 'notes to the accounts' is
therefore probably best dealt with by looking at the many examples of
published charity accounts. However, it would be unwise to produce any

set of charity accounts without having read and thoroughly studied the Schedule to Regulation 3(10), 'Notes to the Accounts'. There are now virtually no differences between the requirements of the regulations and those of the SORP.

The following extract from a Charity Accounts Disclosure Checklist produced by the author for charity clients gives some idea of the areas that need attention.

Have tangible fixed assets been analysed into:	Para. 203
Freehold interests in land and buildings?	
Leasehold and other interests in land and buildings?	
Plant and machinery?	
Fixtures, fittings and equipment?	
Payment on account and assets in the course of construction?	
Are investment assets and income therefrom analysed between:	
Investment properties?	Para. 238(a)
Investments listed on a recognised stock exchange, including ones valued by reference to such investments?	Para. 238(b)
Investments in subsidiary and associated undertakings or in companies that are connected persons?	Para. 238(c)
Other unlisted securities?	Para. 238(d)
Cash held as part of the investment portfolio?	Para. 238(e)
Other?	Para. 238(f)
Where values are determined otherwise than by reference to readily available market prices has the name and qualification of the valuer been given?	Para. 235
Have debtors been analysed into:	Para. 245
Trade debtors?	
Amounts due from subsidiary and associated undertakings	
Other debtors?	
Prepayments	
Accrued income?	

Where there are contingent assets and liabilities has
   the following information been given:
   The amount, or estimated amount?   Para. 266
   Its legal nature?   Para. 267
Is there a description of the nature and purpose of all
   of the charity's significant capital and income funds
   that are subject to legal restrictions as to their use?   Para. 48
Is there an indication whether or not sufficient
   resources are held in an appropriate form to
   enable each fund to be applied in accordance with
   restrictions imposed?   Para. 49(b)
Has the name of each subsidiary and particulars of
   the charity's shareholding, or other controlling
   interest, been given?   Para. 315
Has the number of employees whose emoluments
   fell within each band of £10,000 from £50,000
   upwards been given?   Para. 73
Has the auditor's or independent examiner's
   remuneration been analysed between: Para. 176
   Audit or independent examination services?
   Other services?
Where ex-gratia payments are made otherwise than
   as an application of funds for charitable purposes
   has the total amount or value of the following
   been given: Para. 178
   Payment?
   Non-monetary benefit?
   Other expenditure of any kind?
   Waiver of rights to property to which charity is
      entitled?
Where indemnity insurance has been purchased, is
   that fact and the costs involved given?   Para. 170
Where a trustee or a person with a family or a
   business connection with the trustee has received
   remuneration, directly or indirectly, from either
   the charity or a company which any such persons
   control, has that fact, the name of the recipient,
   the source and the amount been given?   Para. 165

Where trustees have been reimbursed for any
    expenses incurred have the following been stated: Para. 166
    Aggregate amount?
    Nature of the expense?
    Number of trustees reimbursed?
Where gifts in kind have been brought into account
    has the basis of valuation been disclosed?   Para. 97
Has the basis and principles used for the allocation of
    costs been disclosed clearly?   Para. 154
Have particulars of any material departures from the
    SORP and the reasons therefor been given?   Para. 280
Is there an analysis of the major items of the cost of
    generating funds?   Para. 135

The following example again is taken from the author's input into CC66
SORP 2000: Example Reports and Accounts and is for the Arts Theatre
Trust Limited.

Example 8.1

NOTES FORMING PART OF THE FINANCIAL STATEMENTS
FOR THE YEAR ENDED 31 MARCH 2001

1 **Accounting policies**
The financial statements have been prepared under the historical cost basis
and are in accordance with the Statement of Recommended Practice,
Accounting and Reporting by Charities (SORP 2000) issued in October 2000,
applicable accounting standards and the Companies Act 1985. The principle
accounting policies adopted in the preparation of the financial statements are
as follows:

Group financial statements
These financial statements consolidate results of the charity and its wholly
owned subsidiary HTC Limited on a line by line basis. A separate Statement of
Financial Activities, or income and expenditure account, for the charity itself is
not prepared because the charity has taken advantage of the exemptions
provided by section 230 of the Companies Act 1985 and paragraph 304 of
SORP 2000.

Incoming resources
Charitable trading activities
Income from theatre admission fees is included in incoming resources in the period in which the relevant show takes place.

Commercial trading activities
Income from commercial activities is included in the period in which the group is entitled to receipt.

Donations and grants
Income from donations and grants, including capital grants, is included in incoming resources when these are receivable, except as follows:
- When donors specify that donations and grants given to the charity must be used in future accounting periods, the income is deferred until those periods.
- When donors impose conditions which have to be fulfilled before the charity becomes entitled to use such income, the income is deferred and not included in incoming resources until the preconditions for use have been met.

When donors specify that donations and grants, including capital grants, are for particular restricted purposes, which do not amount to preconditions regarding entitlement, this income is included in incoming resources of restricted funds when receivable.

Intangible income
Intangible income, which comprises donated services, is included in income at a valuation which is an estimate of the financial cost borne by the donor where such a cost is quantifiable and measurable. No income is recognised when there is no financial cost borne by a third party.

Interest receivable
Interest is included when receivable by the charity.

Resources expended
Resources expended are included in the Statement of Financial Activities on an accruals basis, inclusive of any VAT which cannot be recovered.

Cost allocation
Certain expenditure is directly attributable to specific activities and has been included in those cost categories. A proportion of staff, establishment and other costs are attributed to costs of generating funds (operating/ trading activities and fundraising), costs of operating the theatre and arts centre and to management and administration costs on an actual time incurred basis.

Pension costs

The charity participates in a defined benefit scheme. Pension costs are assessed in accordance with the advice of the actuaries based on the most recent actuarial valuation of the scheme, accounted for on the basis of charging the cost of providing pensions over the period during which the charity benefits from the employees' services.

Operating leases

Rentals and operating leases are charged to the Statement of Financial Activities as incurred over the term of the lease.

Stock

Stock is stated at the lower of cost or net realisable value. Cost has been calculated on the 'first in, first out' basis. Net realisable value comprises anticipated proceeds of sales less anticipated costs relating thereto.

Tangible fixed assets

All individual fixed assets costing £1,000 or more are capitalised at cost.

The cost of building conversion is depreciated on a straight-line basis over fifty years. The W theatre is depreciated on a straight-line basis over eighty-seven years. Other fixed assets are depreciated on a straight-line basis over their estimated useful lives as follows:

Type of asset	Annual rate
Long leasehold buildings	1%–2%
Plant, equipment and motor vehicles	10%–33%
Pianos	10%

Fund accounting

Funds held by the charity are either:

- restricted – these are funds that can only be used for particular restricted purposes within the objects of the charity. They are incoming resources on which the donor has laid down conditions relating to the expenditure thereon or when funds are specifically raised for particular restricted purposes.
- designated – incoming resources set aside by the trustees out of unrestricted general funds for specific future purposes.
- unrestricted general – incoming resources on which there is no restriction or designation.
- Further explanation of the nature and purpose of each fund is included in the notes to the financial statements.

2 **Legal status of the charity**

The charity is a company limited by guarantee and has no share capital. The liability of each member in the event of winding-up is limited to £5.

3 Incoming resources from operation of the theatre and arts centre

	2001 £'000	2000 £'000
Admission fees	514	489
Public authority services agreements for operation of theatre	509	601
Service agreements with other charities for workshops	154	150
Other income	23	19
	1,200	1,259

4 Operating activities generating funds
The wholly owned trading subsidiary, HTC Limited, which is incorporated in the United Kingdom, distributes its taxable profits to the charity by Gift Aid. A summary of the trading results is shown below. Audited accounts are filed with the Registrar of Companies.

Profit and loss account	2001 £'000	2000 £'000
Turnover	549	146
Cost of sales	(204)	(54)
Gross profit	345	92
Administrative expenses	(126)	(76)
Other income	4	–
Net profit	223	16
Amount given to the Trust	(223)	(16)
Retained in the subsidiary	–	–

HTC Limited operates the bars, restaurant, coffee lounge and all commercial taxable trading operations carried on at the Arts Theatre Trust. The charity owns the entire issued share capital of £1,000 ordinary shares of £1 each.

5 Cost of operation of the theatre and arts centre

	2001	2000
	£'000	£'000
Administration of the box office	152	176
Reception and housekeeping	197	215
Marketing	204	211
Courses	63	58
Central premises costs	191	171
Activities	54	67
Promotions	286	272
SH Park capital project – feasibility study	73	–
Depreciation	66	60
Piano fund	4	–
	1,290	1,230

6 Managing and administering the charity

	2001	2000
	£'000	£'000
Salaries and wages	86	73
Meeting costs	22	6
Legal and professional expenses	19	12
Other costs	25	22
	152	113

7 Staff costs and trustees' remuneration

	2001	2000
	£'000	£'000
Wages and salaries	620	603
Social Security costs	41	39
Ex-gratia payments	16	–
Other pension costs	19	11
	696	653

The ex-gratia payment was made to a former chief executive for whom no pension provision was made. Payment was approved by the Charity Commission on 15 December 2000.

The number of employees earning over £50,000 per annum was nil (2000 – nil).

The trustees received no emoluments or reimbursed expenses during the year.

8 Staff numbers

The average number of full-time equivalent employees (including casual and part-time staff) during the year was made up as follows:

	2001	2000
Arts department	12	9
Administration, marketing and commercial	14	11
Technical	11	10
Bars and coffee shop	21	15
Front of house, box office, cleaning	20	21
Course tutors, models	34	26
	112	92

9 Net movement in funds

	2001 £'000	2000 £'000
This is stated after charging:		
Operating leases – equipment	13	13
Depreciation	66	60
Auditors' remuneration		
– external audit	8	6
– financial consultancy	2	6

10 **Tangible fixed assets – group and charity**

	Long Leasehold £'000	Equipment and motor vehicles £'000	Pianos £'000	Total £'000
Cost				
At 1 April 2000	1,597	869	32	2,498
Additions	–	72	–	72
At 31 March 2001	1,597	941	32	2,570
Depreciation				
At 1 April 2000	845	801	28	1,674
Provided for the year	23	42	1	66
At March 2001	868	843	29	1,740
Net book value				
At 31 March 2001	729	98	3	830
At 31 March 2000	752	68	4	824

11 **Stock**

	Group		Charity	
	2001 £'000	2000 £'000	2001 £'000	2000 £'000
Finished goods for resale	203	212	203	212
Stationery	14	1	–	–
	217	213	203	212

12 **Debtors**

	Group		Charity	
	2001 £'000	2000 £'000	2001 £'000	2000 £'000
Amount due from subsidiary undertaking	–	–	78	–
Taxation	–	–	6	–
Trade debtors	33	20	14	20
Other debtors	119	128	119	128
Prepayments	55	58	55	58
	207	206	272	206

13 Creditors: amount falling due within one year

	Group		Charity	
	2001	2000	2001	2000
	£'000	£'000	£'000	£'000
Trade creditors	67	38	38	38
Other taxes and social security costs	18	19	–	19
Capital grants	53	50	53	50
Other creditors	49	42	39	42
Deferred income (Note 14)	55	46	55	46
	242	195	185	195

14 Deferred income

	Group	Charity
	£'000	£'000
Balance at 1 April 2000	46	49
Amount released to incoming resources	(46)	(49)
Amount deferred in the year	55	46
	55	46

Deferred income comprises admission fees received in advance and grants which the donor has specified must be used in future accounting periods.

15 Creditors: amounts falling due after more than one year

	Group		Charity	
	2001	2000	2001	2000
	£'000	£'000	£'000	£'000
Unsecured loan	46	56	46	56

The loan is provided by XYZ Limited, is interest free and is repayable in equal half-yearly instalments between 2002 and 2007.

16 Unrestricted funds of the charity

	General Fund	Designated Fund	Total
	£'000	£'000	£'000
Balance at 1 April 2000	1,263	31	1,294
Surplus on Statement of Financial Activities	83	–	83
Transfers	(136)	136	–
Balance 31 March 2001	1,210	167	1,377

The income funds of the Charity include designated funds, which have been set aside out of unrestricted funds by the trustees for repairs under the lease of the Arts Theatre.

17 **Restricted funds of the charity**

	Balance 1 April 2000 £'ooo	Incoming resources £'ooo	Balance Outgoing resources £'ooo	31 March 2001 £'ooo
Piano fund	10	3	5	8
Ceramics residency	3	–	3	–
Jazz Course	–	1	1	–
Clay at the park	2	–	–	2
Kennel Ride	2	–	–	2
The Ugly Show	–	1	1	–
AT Capital project	–	73	73	–
	17	78	83	12

The piano fund is for the purchase of a baby grand piano, which was acquired in June 2001.

The Ceramics residency fund is to support the appointment of a resident ceramist. The appointment was made at the beginning of September 2000.

The Jazz course fund is specifically to underwrite the costs of the jazz weekend held in March as an attempt to bring professional and amateur musicians together.

The Clay at the park fund is to publish documents and create an archive relating to the development of clay craft in the Borough.

The Kennel Ride fund is to assist with the Trust's project with the young people of Kennel Ride and with the Btown day care centres for the elderly.

The Ugly Show fund was to underwrite the costs of an exhibition from five artists held in September and October 2000 which explored notions of beauty.

The Arts Council of England gave the Trust a grant of £73,000. This grant was towards the cost of a further feasibility study for alterations, refurbishment and a new extension to the Theatre, which is a Grade 2, listed building. It included the appointment of consultants and the payment of professional fees.

18 **Analysis of group net assets between funds:**

	General Fund £'000	Designated Fund £'000	Restricted Fund £'000	Total £'000
Tangible fixed assets	830	–	–	830
Cash at bank and in hand	244	167	12	423
Other net current assets	182	–	–	182
Long-term liabilities	(46)	–	–	(46)
	1,210	167	12	1,389

19 **Revenue commitments**

The amounts payable in the next year in respect of operating leases shown below, analysed according to the expiry date of the leases.

Equipment	2001 £'000	2000 £'000
One year	1	8
Between two and five years	5	1
	6	9

20 **Related parties**

BF Borough Council a key provider of finance produced revenue of £405,000 to the charity in the year and made a capital grant of £42,000. B Town Council, also a key provider of finance, gave a revenue grant of £104,000 to the charity whilst N Arts made revenue payments of £154,000.

All these payments were made under contract to the charity to provide services, e.g. training in drama production, and have therefore been included in the accounts under the heading *Incoming Resources: from operation of a theatre and arts centre.*

The charity also received a donation in kind, from BF Borough Council, for the rent of premises, which is not included in these financial statements because it could not be quantified because the data can only be extracted by expenditure of unreasonable amounts of time and/or cost.

There were no outstanding balances with related parties at 31 March 2001 (2000 – £0).

21 **Pensions**

The charity operates a funded defined benefit scheme providing benefits based on final remuneration. The assets of the scheme are held separately of those of the charity. The staff are members of the County Pension Fund.

Contributions to the scheme are charged to the SOFA so as to spread the cost of pensions over the employees' working lives with the company. Contributions are determined by a qualified actuary on the basis of valuations using a market related method which derives the financial assumptions by considering various average yields in the twelve months leading up to the valuation date and values the assets of the fund at a value based on the average market value in the twelve months to the valuation date.

The pension charge for the year is £19,000 with a balance outstanding as at 31 March 2001 of £Nil. The assumptions used in the valuation were as follows:

Date of latest actuarial valuation	**31 March 2000**
Investment returns	6.7%–7.2%
Price inflation	3.4%
Earnings increases	5.4%
Market value of assets	£882m
Benefit cover	114%

Other examples

Example 8.1 does not deal with every possible issue and those that are not dealt with are illustrated here.

Indemnity insurance

This is often a particularly contentious subject and many charities are now taking out such insurance. As the earlier checklist has made quite clear, details of this insurance do need to be shown in the notes to the accounts. ActionAid did just this in notes to the financial statements, 31 December 1995, as follows:

'Indemnity insurance is provided for Trustees, directors and officers of ACTIONAID. Premiums paid in 1995 totalled £4,750 (1994: £5,460).'

This does not comply fully with the SORP, but was a move in the right direction. SORP at paragraph 170 says:

If funds belonging to the charity have been used in the purchase of insurance:

a to protect the charity from loss arising from the neglect or defaults of its trustees, employees or agents; or

b to indemnify the trustees or other officers against the conse-quences of any neglect or default on their part;

these facts and the cost involved in providing such insurance should be disclosed in detail in the notes to the accounts.

It might be argued that ActionAid has stated only that the insurance is provided and the premiums that have been paid, whilst not setting out the reasons why.

Investments

Investments are an extremely complex subject due to the changes required by the SORP for many charities in having to account for investments at market value and then deal with realised and unrealised gains and losses. Example 8.2, taken from the accounts of The Royal Society, sets all of this information out in considerable detail:

Example 8.2

ROYAL SOCIETY

NOTES TO THE FINANCIAL STATEMENTS

for the year ended 31 March 1996

	General Purposes Funds £'000	Other Unrestricted Funds £'000	Restricted Funds £'000	Permanent Endowment Funds £'000	1996 Total Funds £'000
Valuation at 1 April 1995 as previously stated	9,276	1,873	12,660	13,917	37,726
Prior Year Adjustment:					
Anonymous Fund	–	–	88	153	241
Horace Le Marquand and Dudley Bigg	–	–	62	–	62
Valuation at 1 April 1995 as restated	9,276	1,873	12,810	14,070	38,029
Additions at cost	3,192	549	3,119	4,847	11,707
Disposals at opening valuation	(3,087)	(462)	(3,186)	(4,509)	(11,244)
Unrealized gains on valuation at 31 March 1996	1,607	310	1,853	2,178	5,948
Valuation at 31 March 1996	10,988	2,270	14,596	16,586	44,440

Comparative figures have been omitted as the data can only be extracted by the expenditure of unreasonable amounts of time and/or cost.

The valuation at 31 March 1996 comprises
Investments listed on a recognised stock
exchange including investments and unit
trusts:

	General Purposes Funds £'000	Other Unrestricted Funds £'000	Restricted Funds £'000	Permanent Endowment Funds £'000	1996 Total Funds £'000	1995 Total Funds (restated) £'000
UK	7,804	1,503	10,836	11,971	32,114	28,880
Overseas	2,884	689	3,206	4,149	10,928	7,101
Cash:						
UK	300	78	554	466	1,398	2,048
	10,988	2,270	14,596	16,586	44,440	38,029
Historical cost						
The historical cost of the investments						
at 31 March 1996 were	8,426	1,759	9,225	13,069	32,479	30,750

At 31 March 1996 91% of the Reckitt Research Fund (Fund value – £2,699k) was invested in the shares of Reckitt & Colman plc. No other investment in any individual share exceeded 5% by value of the total portfolio.

(G18)

Grants

Many of the larger grant-making charities have taken advantage of the
opportunity to reproduce the lists of grants in a separate document as is
the case of the British Heart Foundation who in their accounts for the
year ended 31 March 1995 had the following note:

> 'Liabilities for research and other awards represent the unpaid
> balances on grants awarded as at the balance sheet date. They relate
> to current and ongoing research being funded by the Foundation
> and to which the Foundation is firmly committed.
>
> A list of awards made during the year can be found in the
> Annual Review which accompanies this Annual Report, or is
> obtainable from The Secretary, British Heart Foundation, 14
> Fitzhardinge Street, London W1H 4DH.'

9   Summary Financial Information and Statements

Introduction

Summary financial information and statements are those derived from the full annual accounts of the charity and expressed in any form, for example extracts, graphs, tables, etc., which purport to be, or represent, the accounts of the charity. These accounts often form part of a document produced by the charity and described as the 'annual report', but more correctly described as the 'annual review' as it does not contain all the information required by law.

Such forms of the accounts, where produced by charities, have to be approved formally by the trustees and accompanied by a statement from the charity's auditors that they are consistent and accurate by reference to the full detailed accounts. Many charities issue publicity material that contains accounts information, often highly abbreviated and partly in graphical or other pictorial form. Such information has to follow the rules laid out in the revised SORP (paragraphs 292–7).

Content

Obviously, the purpose of these summarised accounts may be quite different, dependent on the type of charity preparing them and the reasons for their preparation e.g. to raise funds, to inform the public about the activities of the charity, etc. The revised SORP makes it clear that as the style will vary considerably from charity to charity it is not practicable to give detailed recommendations on the content. It does, however, set out some general principles (SORP, paragraph 293). The full annual report and accounts must always be produced irrespective of the circulation of any summary financial information or statement. Thus, even if all interested parties receive a copy of the summary financial information the full report and accounts must be available (SORP, paragraph 294).

All such abbreviated accounts should be accompanied by a statement signed on behalf of the trustees explaining that they are a summary of information extracted from the annual accounts and they should contain information which relates both to the SOFA and the balance sheet (SORP, paragraph 295). All summarised accounts should state the date on which the annual accounts, of which they are a summary, were approved. In addition, for those charities registered in England and Wales it will also be necessary to state whether the full annual report and accounts have been submitted to the Charity Commission (SORP, paragraph 295).

If branch accounts are produced, it must clearly be stated that the summary is for the branch only and has been extracted from the full accounts of the main charity, giving the name of that charity. The summary financial information and statements should also give details of how the full annual accounts, the external examiners report (as applicable) and the Trustees' Report can be obtained.

Audit/independent examination

The statement that accompanies the summarised accounts must also show clearly whether or not the full annual accounts have at the date of issuing the statement been audited or independently examined for unincorporated charities and audited or received an audit exemption report for incorporated charities (SORP, paragraph 295). In those cases where they have been, there has to be a statement from the auditor or independent examiner giving their opinion as to whether or not the summarised accounts are consistent with the full accounts (SORP, paragraph 296). The Auditing Practices Board's Practice Note 11, The Audit of Charities, currently being reviewed (see further Chapter 13), gives the example shown below.

Example 9.1

AUDITORS' STATEMENT TO THE TRUSTEES OF XYZ CHARITY

We have examined the summarised financial statements set out in pages ... to ...

Respective responsibilities of trustees and auditors
You are responsible as trustees for the preparation of the summary financial statements. We have agreed to report to you our opinion on the summarised statements' consistency with the full financial statements, on which we reported to you on (date).

Basis of opinion

We have carried out the procedures we consider necessary to ascertain whether the summarised financial statements are consistent with the full financial statements from which they have been prepared.

Opinion

In our opinion the summarised financial statements are consistent [are not consistent] with the full financial statements for the year ended 31 December 19xx [in the following respects ...]

Registered auditors ....

Address ....

Date ....

This statement will also have to make it clear whether the full accounts were unqualified or not (SORP, paragraph 295). If the report and accounts were qualified then the statement accompanying the summarised accounts should give enough details to enable the reader to appreciate the significance of the qualification. However, a full repeat of the auditor's or independent examiner's report will not be necessary (SORP, paragraph 295). Summarised accounts prepared and produced by an incorporated charity will have no legal status, that is to say, they will not be the statutory accounts.

The statutory requirements for the publication of summary financial statements only applies to public companies, therefore the auditors' report cannot be published with the summarised accounts as it must be attached to the statutory accounts to which it relates.

Incorporated charities

Charitable companies have to follow these recommendations and in addition must make clear in the accompanying statement whether or not the accounts have been sent to the Registrar of Companies (SORP, paragraph 292).

Other summary financial information

The SORP, paragraph 297 makes it clear that any other summary financial information in whatever form it is produced which does not include information on the SOFA and the balance sheet must be accompanied by a statement signed on behalf of the trustees showing clearly the:

'• purpose of the information;
• whether or not it is from the full accounts;
• whether or not these accounts have been audited, independently examined or subject to a reporting accounts report;
• details of how the full annual accounts, trustees report and external examiners/audit report (as appropriate) can be obtained.'

Full accounts

Even if all interested parties, that is, stakeholders, do receive a copy of the summary financial statements, the full report and accounts must still be made available if requested. However, for many charities, because of their governing document, there may well be a legal requirement to supply, for example to their members, copies of the full accounts. Therefore, such charities will not be able to rely just on issuing to those members the summarised version, that is to say, the summary financial statements.

Examples of summary financial information and statements

More and more charities are as a result of the 1995 SORP issuing summarised accounts and summary financial statements and the two examples that follow have been prepared on the basis of that SORP. The first example is of an extract from a review produced by the charity Changing Faces that included some summarised figures. The second example is extracted from a publication issued by the Engineering Construction Industry Training Board, which was approved by the Secretary of State for Trade and Industry.

Example 9.2

CHANGING FACES

Report and Accounts 15

Financial Report, Year Ended 31 March 1996

Income and Expenditure Account

Income	Year ended 31 March 1996	Year ended 31 March 1995
Trust income	195,591	136,440
Private donations	17,215	6,566
Corporate donations	61,450	38,900
Grants receivable	51,617	20,290
Other income	21,664	11,476
Total	347,537	213,672
Expenditure		
Work with adults	53,609	43,127
Work with children	39,715	19,474
Information service	45,926	8,323
New initiatives	97,845	51,321
Support costs	25,069	14,523
Fundraising and publicity	32,487	23,445
Administration	27,796	17,043
Total	322,447	177,256
Income less expenditure	25,090	36,416

Balance sheet	As at 31 March 1996	As at 31 March 1995
Tangible assets	41,737	3,298
Current assets	146,632	104,613
Less current liabilities	−30,751	−3,295
Less creditors due after more than one year	−27,912	
Total net assets	129,706	104,616
Represented by:		
Income and Expenditure Account	**£129,706**	**£104,616**

Changing Faces is a company limited by guarantee, not for profit and not having a share capital divided into shares. The statutory reports and accounts are in the format required by the Companies Act 1985. The accounts, which were audited by Moores Rowland and received unqualified audit reports, are available on request. The annual accounts were approved by the Board on 30 July 1996. The accounts have been filed at the Charity Commission and at Companies House. Full accounts are available on request.

Example 9.3

Extract from Engineering Construction Industry Training Board annual report and financial statements 1996

FINANCIAL REVIEW

Finance 1996
In common with good commercial practice, the Board put out to tender the audit of the Board and Moores Rowland, chartered accountants and registered auditors, were selected in succession to Deloitte & Touche. It is felt that Moores Rowland offer best value for money whilst having the capability to provide expertly all the relevant services required by the Board. The Board is indebted to Deloitte & Touche, the retiring auditors, for their valued services over a number of years.

The financial statements have been prepared in accordance with the provisions of the Statement of Recommended Practice (SORP) 'Accounting by Charities', so there has been some revision of the presentation and information.

The summary financial statement shown on page 27 has been extracted from the audited annual financial statements; the auditors' report thereon is unqualified. The summary financial statement may not contain sufficient information to allow for a full understanding of the financial affairs of the Board. For further information the full financial statements and reports, including the auditors' report, for the year to 31 December 1996 are available upon written request to the Board Secretary.

Signed on behalf of the Board
P.J. Griffiths
Director/Chief Executive

FINANCIAL REVIEW

Citizen's Charter and Open Government

Non-Departmental Public Bodies, of which the ECITB is one, are required to apply Citizen's Charter principles. The aims of the Charter are to raise the standards of public service and make them more responsive to the wishes of the users.

As can be seen from the statement in the Board's Strategic Plan and from this report generally, the ECITB is constantly seeking to ensure that its policies accord with the industry's needs and that it operates cost effectively in the interests of its levy payers.

At a meeting of the Board approval was given to a Code of Best Practice for its Board members, based on HM Treasury Code of Practice published in 1997. The Board also approved a Code of Practice on Access to Information, prepared in accordance with the Government's Code of Practice on

Access to Government Information published in 1994 under the Citizen's Charter. Both of these Codes of Practice also comply with the relevant recommendations of the Nolan Committee on Standards in Public Life.

Policy on Prompt Payment

The ECITB's payment policy observes the principles of the CBI's Code –

Prompt Payers Code, including monitoring payment performance which indicates that accounts rendered by suppliers are settled on average on or before the 22nd working day following receipt of an invoice and that queries on accounts rendered are resolved as expeditiously as possible.

Auditors' statement to the Board Officials of the Engineering Construction Industry Training Board

We have examined the summary financial statement set out on page 27.

Respective responsibilities of officials and auditors

The summary financial statement is the responsibility of the Board's officials. Our responsibility is to report to you our opinion on its preparation and consistency with the full report and financial statements.

Basis of opinion

We conducted our work in accordance with the Auditing Guideline 'The auditors' statement on the summary financial statement' adopted by the Auditing Practices Board.

Opinion

In our opinion the summary financial statement is consistent with the full report and financial statements of the Engineering Construction Industry Training Board for the year ended 31 December 1996 and complies with the requirements of the Statement of Recommended Practice 'Accounting by Charities', and regulations made thereunder, applicable to summary financial statements.

Moores Rowland
Chartered Accountants
and Registered Auditors
19 March 1997

Summary Financial Statement for the year to 31 December 1996
Abbreviated Balance Sheet

At 31.12.95 £000		At 31.12.96 £000
	Fixed assets	
949	Tangible assets	905
4,333	Investments	5,722
10,913	Current assets less creditors	9,133
16,195	Total assets less current liabilities	15,760
(300)	Provision for liabilities and charges	(300)
15,895	Unrestricted fund	15,460

Summarised Statement of Financial Activities

Year to 31.12.95 £000		Year to 31.12.96 £000
10,365	Levy receivable	9,445
2,709	Investment income, grant and initiative support and other operating income	2,833
13,074	Total incoming resources	12,278
11,463	Training grants and initiatives	11,687
841	Management and administration	909
50	Redundancy and severance costs	34
–	Notional cost of capital	1,217
12,354	Total resources expended and notional cost of capital	13,847
720	Net (outgoing)/incoming resources for the year after notional cost of capital	(1,569)
–	Notional cost of capital	1,217
415	Unrealised (losses)/gains on investment assets	(83)
1,135	Net movement in funds	(435)
14,760	Balance brought forward at 1 January	15,895
15,895	Balance carried forward at 31 December	15,460

Conclusion

Unfortunately, too many charities are still producing incorrect summarised information. Therefore, greater care must *be* taken in producing these, now that the SORP and regulations are more fully effective. Where a charity wishes to include summary financial information and statements in its publications, it can choose the format in which it wishes to present the financial information but it would be advisable to follow certain general principles since this information:

- cannot be the only form of accounts produced by the charity for the year;
- should always be accompanied by a statement that they are only an extract;
- should include information relating to both the SOFA and the balance sheet for summary financial statements;
- should state the date on which the full accounts were approved;
- should indicate whether the full accounts have been audited/independently examined;
- should indicate whether the report is qualified or unqualified; and
- should state whether a copy of the full accounts has been sent to the Charity Commission and, if appropriate, the Registrar of Companies.

10 Consolidation of Subsidiary Undertakings

Introduction

Much confusion has arisen over the question of whether or not to consolidate. There is probably even more confusion caused by the fact that some advisers use the word consolidation incorrectly to cover such things as the incorporation of a charity's branch accounts into the main accounts of the charity. Unless the branch is autonomous the incorporation is not a consolidation but merely the correct accounting treatment for one legal entity. The inclusion of the results of a trading subsidiary on the other hand, which is a separate legal entity, is a consolidation.

Consolidated accounts for a charity and any subsidiary undertakings that it might have comprise an additional set of financial statements supplementing the parent charity's own accounts. The purpose is to present a true and fair view of the state of affairs and activities of the charity and its subsidiary undertakings as a whole (SORP, paragraph 229). A parent charity should prepare consolidated accounts including all its subsidiary undertakings except where:

- The gross income of the group in the accounting period is no more than the audit threshold under the Charities Act 1993.
- The subsidiary undertaking or undertakings results are not material to the group.
- The accounts have to be aggregated under charity legislation in England and Wales.

1988 SORP 2 recommendations

Charities traditionally accounted for their trading subsidiaries in a variety of ways. In some cases they consolidated the accounts of the subsidiary on a line-by-line basis and in other cases on a one-line basis, that is, net. Many charities prepared full group accounts on consolidation, and even those that did it on a single line in the income and expenditure account produced a fully consolidated balance sheet. It is probably true to say that most charities with subsidiary undertakings, from 1988 to 1996, followed the recommendations of SORP 2, which stated:

'A charity may have one or more subsidiary companies.

a   The activities of a subsidiary may not be fundamentally different from those of the charity. For example, the subsidiary may be an investment holding company; it might be concerned solely or largely with fundraising; or it might be the vehicle used to undertake the charitable activities of the charity. If a charity has such a subsidiary or subsidiaries, it should prepare consolidated accounts for itself and its subsidiary or subsidiaries. Separate accounts for the charity itself should still be prepared.

b   If a subsidiary undertakes activities that are fundamentally different from those of the charity, for example if it is a trading company, it will not be appropriate to consolidate its accounts with those of the charity. Instead, the investment in the subsidiary should be treated in the same way that other investments are treated. A summary of the transactions, assets and liabilities of the subsidiary, together with an explanation of its activities and their relevance to the charity, should be disclosed in the notes to the accounts. As an alternative to providing a summary of its subsidiary's transactions, assets and liabilities, the charity may if it wishes include the accounts of the subsidiary within its annual report.'

1989 Companies Act

This Act, which was published after SORP 2, introduced several significant changes that considerably reduce the number of reasons for excluding a subsidiary from consolidated accounts. Therefore, charities, which were incorporated and for which as we have seen the Companies Act took precedence, had to reconsider their policy on consolidation if they had previously excluded the subsidiary undertaking(s).

Most charity groups probably fall within the Companies Act definition of parent and subsidiary undertakings, even in cases where the charity does not own the majority of the shares of the subsidiary. Most frequently in these cases, the charity will still be in a position to control the trading subsidiary by the right to appoint its directors and organise its administration (Companies Act 1985, s. 258). In these cases, the general requirements of sections 227 and 229 of the Companies Act, which require consolidated accounts including all subsidiaries to be prepared, would have to be followed. Historically, many charities have not consolidated their trading subsidiaries, using the excuse that the sums involved were not material or, more commonly, that the activities were totally dissimilar, for example, the charity's income came from donations whilst the trading subsidiary's came from sales.

The Companies Act, s. 229(2) allows the exclusion of subsidiaries from consolidation provided that the inclusion of all such subsidiaries is not material to giving a true and fair view. Whilst this may be sufficient for commercial organisations, it is often the case that because of charities' public image, the fundraising aspects and the fact that the public's money is involved, it would be detrimental to exclude from consolidation these trading subsidiaries even where they are not material.

In summary, an undertaking is a parent undertaking to a subsidiary undertaking if:

a   it holds a majority of the voting rights in the subsidiary undertaking;

b   it is a member of the subsidiary undertaking and has the right to appoint or remove a majority of its Board of Directors;

c   it has the right to exercise a dominant influence over the subsidiary undertaking by virtue of:

d   provisions contained in the subsidiary undertaking's Memorandum or Articles; or

e   a control contract;

f   it is a member of the subsidiary undertaking and controls, alone, pursuant to an agreement with other shareholders or members, a majority of the voting rights in the undertaking; or

g   it has a participating interest in the undertaking and:

   i   it actually exercises a dominant influence over it; or

   ii   it and the subsidiary undertaking are managed on a unified basis.

Financial Reporting Standard (FRS) 2

FRS 2 sets out the conditions under which an organisation qualifies as a 'undertaking' which should prepare consolidated financial statements for its group, the parent and its subsidiaries. It also sets out the manner in which consolidated financial statements are to be prepared. The SORP, paragraphs 299–319 explains consolidation and the applicability of FRS 2 to charities (see below, pp. 104–7).

FRS 2 applies to all parent undertakings and requires compliance so that those preparing accounts in this way will produce a consolidated financial statement which is intended to give a true and fair view of the financial position and profit or loss (or income and expenditure). The FRS defines an undertaking as:

> 'A body corporate or partnership, or an unincorporated association carrying on a trade or business with or without a view to profit.'

Therefore, although only charities that are incorporated will be caught by the Companies Act, FRS 2 will effectively pick up all entities, whether incorporated or not, preparing true and fair view accounts. FRS 2 states that:

> 'a The consolidated financial statements should be prepared by consolidating financial information for the parent undertaking and all its subsidiary undertakings, except for any subsidiary undertakings that are to be excluded from consolidation by virtue of the requirements of the Act and the FRS.
>
> b A subsidiary undertaking is to be excluded from consolidation if:
>
>> i severe long-term restrictions substantially hinder the exercise of the parent undertaking's rights over the subsidiary undertaking's assets or management; or
>>
>> ii the group's interest in the subsidiary undertaking is held exclusively with a view to subsequent resale and the subsidiary undertaking has not previously been consolidated; or
>>
>> iii the subsidiary undertaking's activities are so different from those of other undertakings to be included in the consolidation that its inclusion will be incompatible with the obligation to give a true and fair view.'

FRS 2 allows subsidiaries to be excluded from consolidation in certain very limited circumstances. However, it is unlikely that these exclusions will apply to a charitable group, except on very rare occasions. The difference between profit and not-for-profit undertakings is not sufficient of itself to justify non-consolidation. However, where a subsidiary under-taking is a registered company, is insolvent and being wound up, then the subsidiary undertaking can be excluded from the consolidation.

Revised SORP

Consolidated accounts for a charity and any subsidiary undertakings that it might have comprise an additional set of financial statements supplementing the parent charity's own accounts. The purpose is to present a true and fair view of the state of affairs and activities of the charity and its subsidiary undertakings as a whole (SORP, paragraph 299). Having looked briefly at what the Companies Act and FRS 2 have to say about these, what does the SORP spell out about the consolidation of subsidiary undertakings? The Glossary, whilst referring the reader to the Companies Act 1985, ss. 258 and 259, makes it clear that:

> 'In relation to a charity an undertaking is the parent undertaking of another undertaking, a subsidiary undertaking where the charity or its trustees hold or control the majority of the voting rights, or have the right to appoint or remove a majority of the board of directors or trustees of the subsidiary undertaking, or have the right to exercise a dominant influence over the subsidiary undertaking.'

It continues:

> 'Paragraphs 299 to 319 explain how to account for subsidiary undertakings within the consolidated accounts of a parent undertaking. This includes the exemptions from consolidation and the particular circumstances in which a charity can be considered to be a subsidiary undertaking of another charity.'

Purpose and scope

As the revised SORP sets out a parent charity should always prepare consolidated accounts including all its subsidiary undertakings unless:

'a The gross income of the group in the accounting period is no more than the audit threshold under the Charities Act 1993 which can be revised by Ministerial Order;

b The subsidiary undertaking or undertakings results are not material to the group;

c The accounts have to be aggregated under the charity legislation in England and Wales.'

Although FRS 2 allows subsidiaries to be excluded from consolidation in some very limited circumstances it is unlikely that these exclusions will apply to a charitable group. In the case of the subsidiary undertaking of a charity being a non-company charity then it should be accounted for in the same manner as a branch would be, that is, its results should be incorporated into the accounts in full (SORP, paragraphs 51–5).

In the same way, those charities, whether they happen to be companies or not, that use non-charitable subsidiary undertakings to carry out their charitable purposes should prepare consolidated accounts for the charity and any such subsidiary undertakings (SORP, paragraph 302). Consolidated accounts must be prepared under accounting standards in order to give a true and fair view of the group. Individual accounts for each member of the group – parent and subsidiary undertakings – should be prepared for approval by the respective boards of trustees and/or directors. Then consolidated group accounts should be prepared by the parent company.

To meet the requirements of the Charities Act 1993, in England and Wales, the individual charity's accounts have to be filed with the Charity Commission. This can cause problems as most frequently in consolidated accounts whilst there are usually two balance sheets, one consolidated and the other just for the charity, more often than not there are not two separate Statements of Financial Activities. The most likely case is that there will be only one SOFA covering the group. The Charity Commission is prepared to accept these accounts, which effectively omit the parent charity SOFA, as long as the assets and liabilities of the charity can be separately distinguished from those of its subsidiary undertaking(s) and that the turnover and results of the subsidiary undertaking(s) are clearly stated.

It should be noted however that the Charity Commission obviously still has the power to require the production and filing of any individual charity's SOFAs and similarly any members of the public have a legal right to request a copy of the individual charity's SOFA.

Method of consolidation

As previously mentioned consolidation should be done on a line-by-line basis as set out in FRS 2 applying the normal rules (SORP, paragraph 309). In other words all items of incoming resources and resources expended should be shown gross and netting off should not occur. It is also felt desirable that similar items should be treated in exactly the same way. As the SORP, paragraph 310 puts it:

'For instance operating activities for generating funds in the charity should be combined with similar activities in the subsidiary, and charitable activities within the charity should be combined with charitable activities in the subsidiary. Similarly costs of generating funds and/or administration costs in the subsidiary should be aggregated with those of the charity.'

It is down to individual charities to choose appropriate line headings within the permissible format of the SOFA and these headings should be expanded and changed to reflect the underlying activities of the group (SORP, paragraph 311). In those cases where it is not possible to find exactly matching items between the parent charity and the subsidiary undertaking then segmental information should be provided so that the results of the parent charity and each subsidiary undertaking can be clearly understood (SORP, paragraph 318).

Additionally, as far as a balance sheet is concerned, there should be a full consolidation, i.e. assets and liabilities of all subsidiaries should be consolidated on a line-by-line basis.

Disclosure requirements

Charitable activities carried out by a subsidiary should be consolidated on a line-by-line basis with those of the charity. Other and non-charitable activities should be consolidated by segregating and summarising the results of the trading by gross incoming resources and resources expended. The notes to the accounts should distinguish the assets, liabilities, turnover and profit or loss of the trading subsidiary from those of the charity. Consolidation should follow the principles set out in FRS 2.

There should be a separate comment in the Trustees' Annual Report concerning the performance of the charity's subsidiary undertakings. Where consolidated accounts have been prepared then the method of consolidation should be stated in the policy notes setting out which subsidiary undertakings or associated companies are included or excluded from the consolidation. In general, the notes to the consolidated accounts should give the position of the group as well as the parent undertaking. These notes should state the aggregate amount of the total investment of the charity in its subsidiary undertakings.

Where a charity has a large number of subsidiary undertakings such that this disclosure would result in information of excessive length being given then the information need only be given in respect of those undertakings whose results or financial position materially affect the figures shown in the charity's annual accounts. In consolidated accounts funds or reserves retained by subsidiary undertakings other than funds used in carrying out the charity's objects should be included under an appropriate separate fund heading in the balance sheet.

Consolidation checklist	SORP (paragraph)
Subsidiaries used for charitable purposes	
Charities use subsidiaries (and other charity or company) for charitable purposes.	302
If subsidiary is a charity it will normally be accounted for as a branch of main charity.	302
If parent charity and a subsidiary are charitable companies – consolidated accounts.	302
If charity (whether company or not) used non-charitable subsidiary to carry out its charitable purposes then consolidated accounts required for charity and its subsidiaries regardless of the size of group.	302
Normal rules of method of consolidation apply under FRS 2 – line by line basis.	304
Subsidiaries used for other purposes	
Where trading takes place and profit passed to parent charity then consolidated accounts to be prepared in all cases under FRS 2.	
Where subsidiary carries out fundraising then best presented in charity group accounts as separate line on the consolidated SOFA supported by a note.	
Where subsidiary undertakings are excluded or consolidated accounts are not prepared the trustees should explain reasons for not consolidating in a note to the accounts.	317

Accounting for associated undertakings

FRS 9 sets out the definitions and accounting treatments for associates, joint ventures and joint arrangements. Its also provides detailed guidance on how to determine the relationship between the entities involved. The FRS also deals with the joint arrangements that are not entities. The revised SORP, paragraphs 320–30, explain the applicability of FRS 9 to charities. Again in all cases consolidated accounts should be prepared subject to the exemptions set out in SORP, paragraph 300.

Where a charity has a long-term participating interest in another undertaking and exercises significant influence over its operating and financial policy then this is likely to be an associate undertaking. In a joint venture situation a separate entity is jointly controlled by two or more undertakings all of which have a say in the operation of the joint venture so that no one investing undertaking controls the joint venture but all together can do so. Often, charities undertake joint arrangements where they may carry out activities in partnership with other bodies but without establishing a separate legal entity.

Whether or not consolidated accounts have been prepared covering a charity's subsidiary undertakings(s), any interest that the charity has in associated undertakings has to be fully reported. The method of reporting is set out in the revised SORP, paragraphs 325–8 and, to quote from paragraph 325:

> 'Associates should be included in the accounts based on the net equity method. The consolidated Statement of Financial Activities should show the net interest in the results for the year in the associates as a separate line after the 'net incoming/(resources expended)' line. In the balance sheet the net interest in associates should be shown as a separate line within fixed asset investments.'

To comply with FRS 9 the trustees should provide in a note to the charity's accounts the following information in relation to each associate and joint venture in which it has a participating interest:

a   its name;
b   particulars of the charity's shareholding or other interest in it;
c   the nature of the activities of the associate or joint venture;
d   the charity's interest in the results showing separately its share in:
    i   gross incoming resources by type;
    ii   cost of generating funds;
    iii   expenditure on charitable activities;
    iv   expenditure on management and administration;

v   the net results (where tax is payable the share of the results pre and post tax and the share in the tax should be shown);

vi   gains or losses on investments and the share in unrealised gains on other fixed assets;

vii   fixed assets;

viii   current assets;

ix   liabilities under one year;

x   liabilities over one year;

xi   the different funds of the charity;

xii   contingent liabilities and other commitments;

xiii   particulars of any qualifications contained in any audit or other statutory report on its accounts, and any note or reservation in those accounts to call attention to a matter which, apart from the note or reservations, would properly have been referred to in such a qualification.

The SORP makes clear that where a charity holds 20 per cent or more of the voting rights in any form of undertaking it will be presumed to have a significant influence over the operating and financial policy of the undertaking unless something to the contrary is shown. In all these cases then the undertaking will be considered to be an associated undertaking (SORP, paragraph 322).

Examples

Despite the recommendations of the 1995 SORP there were still a variety of ways of dealing with (trading) subsidiaries which charities have adopted. This is probably because of the anomalies within the 1995 SORP itself, particularly in relation to trading activities. However, it is probably true to say that more and more charities are in fact moving towards a full consolidation for all trading subsidiaries. As an example, the notes to the accounts of the Disabled Drivers' Association clearly state:

'The group accounts consolidate the accounts of DDA Enterprises Ltd.'

Whilst those for the Yorkshire Cancer Research Campaign on the topic of the basis of consolidation say:

'Group accounts have been prepared in respect of the Campaign and its wholly owned subsidiary undertaking, YCRC Cards Ltd. As permitted by Section 230 of the Companies Act 1985 a separate profit and loss account for the parent company is not presented.' This has further been reinforced in CC62 SORP 2000: *Example Reports and Accounts* which in the introduction makes the points that:

The examples include consolidation of subsidiary undertakings, which are trading entities to raise funds for the charity itself. They are not carrying out charitable activities. Therefore, all the costs of the subsidiary are included as 'costs of generating funds'. If, on the other hand, the subsidiary were carrying out some of the charity's activities on its behalf a proportion of the expenditure of the subsidiary might be shown in the consolidated accounts as charitable expenditure within the classifications specified by paragraph 60 (ii) of SORP 2000.

The examples have assumed that there are no intra-group charges, which require elimination, for example rents charged to a trading subsidiary by a charity, would be eliminated on consolidation.

A separate Statement of Financial Activities has not been *presented* for the charity itself in any of the examples of consolidated financial statements as reliance is being placed on exemptions available in the Companies Act 1985 and in paragraph 304 of SORP 2000. However, paragraph 304 of the SORP does not exempt the charity from *preparing* a SOFA for itself as an individual entity and the Charity Commission retains the power to require the production and filing of any individual charity Statement of Financial Activities and similarly members of the public have a legal right to request this Statement.

Conclusion

Historically, many charities have consolidated the results of their trading activities but there have been a number of others that did not do so on the grounds of either immateriality or difference of operation. These reasons for exclusion were no longer permitted by the 1995 Charities SORP. Therefore, this led to some charities having to consolidate the results of their trading subsidiaries for the first time. This in fact was a relatively straightforward exercise and for many charities there have been no problems, or very few. However, as we have seen, for some charities with substantial retail operations compliance with the SORP has caused difficulties.

As a result of the revised SORP it will no longer be possible to do a one line (netting off) consolidation and all consolidations must be done in full (gross line by line).

11   Charitable Companies

Introduction

This chapter sets out the position of the revised SORP on charitable companies. Where charities follow the revised SORP they will normally meet most of the reporting requirements under the Companies Act. Be warned, however, that the SORP does not reproduce in full those requirements and a charity must look at the Companies Act 1985 therefore (SORP, paragraph 331). There are certain requirements that need to be met by charitable companies in addition to following the main sections of the revised SORP. These are commented on in detail below.

Charities that are registered as companies must file an annual report with their accounts at Companies House. Unless they are excepted from registration they must also file an annual report and accounts with the Charity Commission if their income or expenditure exceeds £10,000, or if the Commission asks them for that information. In such cases the accounts are prepared under Companies Acts requirements. Although annual report requirements for charities and companies are different, it is possible to produce one report that will meet both sets of report requirements. The revised SORP applies to charities (unless a more specialised SORP such as the one for housing associations applies), whether they are companies or not. The Charity Commission's powers to investigate and to protect charitable property also apply to charities, whether or not they are companies.

Charities registered in Scotland and Northern Ireland are not governed by the Charities Act 1993 or the regulations and will not, therefore, be monitored by the Charity Commission, nor will they need to make returns to it.

Accounts and reports

Obviously charitable companies need to comply with the Companies Act 1985 with respect to the form and content of their accounts. Additionally

there will be the need to produce a directors' report but the Charity
Commission are prepared to accept that report provided it also meets the
requirements of Part VI of the Charities Act 1993 for a trustees' report
(SORP, paragraph 332). Charitable companies must always include the
names of all the directors in their annual report and unlike non-company
charities do not have an exemption from this requirement.

In cases where the charity is incorporated it is recommended that the
requirements of the directors' report are covered in the trustees' report. It
will certainly be possible to produce one report covering both the requirements of the relevant Charities and Companies Acts. An example of this
is that shown in the report of The Mental Health Foundation (a company
limited by guarantee) for the year ended 31 March 1997 which reads as
follows:

> 'Statement of the Trustees' responsibilities in respect of the Accounts
> The Trustees are required to prepare accounts for each financial
> year which give a true and fair view of the state of affairs of the
> Foundation and of the surplus or deficit of the Foundation for that
> period. Preparing those accounts, the Trustees are required to:
> - select suitable accounting policies and then apply them consis-
>   tently; make judgements and estimates that are reasonable and
>   prudent;
> - state whether applicable accounting standards have been
>   followed, subject to any material departures disclosed and
>   explained in the accounts; and
> - prepare the accounts on the going concern basis unless it is
>   inappropriate to resume that the Foundation will continue in
>   business.
> - The Trustees are responsible for keeping proper accounting
>   records which disclose with reasonable accuracy at any time the
>   financial position of the Foundation and to enable them to
>   ensure that the accounts comply with the Companies Act 1985.
>   They are also responsible for safeguarding the assets of the
>   Foundation and hence for taking reasonable steps for the
>   prevention and detection of fraud and other irregularities.'

Some charitable companies make this further self explanatory by
including the word 'directors' wherever the word 'Trustees' appears,
others somewhat unfortunately omit the word 'Trustees' and only refer to
'directors'. Given that they are primarily charities first and companies

second, this is indeed a mistake and it is vital to ensure that the word 'trustees' is always used.

The requirement to show a true and fair view and to adapt the accounts to the special nature of a charity means that there is a strong presumption that charitable companies will in all but exceptional circumstances have to comply with the revised SORP in order to meet the requirements of company law. Paragraph 3.(3) of part 1, section A of Schedule 4 to the Companies Act 1985 requires, as the revised SORP puts it, 'the directors to adapt the headings and sub-headings of the balance sheet and profit and loss account in any case where the special nature of the company' business requires such adaption (SORP, paragraph 333).

Particulars of any material departures from the SORP must be disclosed (SORP, paragraph 280). A departure is not justified simply because it gives the reader a more appealing picture to the financial position or results of the charity (SORP, paragraph 334).

SOFA and the Summary Income and Expenditure Account

Certain charities may be required by law to prepare income and expenditure accounts, for example Scottish charities (which are not monitored by the Charity Commission) and charities incorporated under the Companies Act. Where a charity has capital funds, e.g. permanent endowment, where there have been receipts during the year which are shown in the SOFA then these will not be part of income to be reported in an income and expenditure account. In these cases the charity will certainly have to produce a simple statutory income and expenditure account with the SOFA providing the detailed information. Where there are no such movements then the SOFA will incorporate the income and expenditure account.

All charitable companies registered under the Companies Act must include an income and expenditure account in their financial statements. The SOFA is designed to include all the gains and losses of a charity that would be found in the income and expenditure account and the statement of total recognised gains and losses as required by FRS 3. A separate income and expenditure account is therefore not necessarily required, however, if it cannot be separately recognised within the SOFA or where there are items which may be open to challenge if included in an income and expenditure account then a separate income and expenditure account should be produced (SORP, paragraph 335).

Items that may be open to challenge if shown in an income and expenditure account include:

- movement on endowment (capital funds) during the year;
- unrealised gains and losses arising during the year.

Whilst unrealised gains and losses are not allowed to be shown in an income and expenditure account, most of these are included in the SOFA as a separate section which would not form part of a conventional income and expenditure account as is explained in the following paragraph.

Where the SOFA does not include items open to challenge then it may not need to produce a separate summary income and expenditure account but the headings in the SOFA must clearly indicate that it does include an income and expenditure account and a statement of total recognised gains and losses (where required). Care must also be taken to ensure that all realised gains and losses are included in the SOFA in such a way that they fall within the bounds of the headings for an income and expenditure account (SORP, paragraph 336). It should be stressed that in those rare cases where there are impairment losses (or reversals thereof) particular attention needs to be paid to their treatment in the accounts to ensure that the guidance in FRS 11 is followed. (See further SORP, paragraphs 224–30.)

Where a summary income and expenditure account is required it should be derived from and cross-referenced to the corresponding figures in the SOFA. Whilst it need not distinguish between unrestricted and restricted income funds the accounting basis on which the items are included must be the same as in the SOFA (SORP, paragraph 337). It should show separately in respect of continuing operations acquisitions and discontinued operations:

a gross income from all sources;

b net gains/losses from disposals of all fixed assets belonging to the charity's income funds;

c transfers from endowment funds of amounts previously received as capital resources and now converted into income funds for expending;

d total income (this will be the total of all incoming resources – other than revaluation gains – of all the income funds but not for any endowment funds);

e total expenditure out of the charity's income funds; and

f net income or expenditure for the year.

Where consolidated accounts are prepared a summary income and expenditure account should be included for the group when it is required (SORP, paragraph 338).

In order to comply with Schedule 4 to the Companies Act, a charity would be expected to show the total income, the surplus or deficit (before tax) and any transfer to reserves in the summarised income and expenditure account. However, the position in Scotland is somewhat different and the regulations for charities there would require more information in the statutory income and expenditure account.

As we have seen, however, in most cases, there will probably be no new permanent endowment or capital funds being introduced into the charity. In this case, the SOFA will include only income and will be the same as an income and expenditure account as far as the first part is concerned. Therefore, with very minute adaptations to the terminology, the requirements to produce an income and expenditure account should be met without having to produce a separate summary income and expenditure account.

Example 3 in Appendix 4 of the 1995 SORP showed how the summary income and expenditure account should be drawn up in the then prescribed format. In practice this format may well need to be modified to comply with specific statutory requirements or those of the charity's own governing document. One example, taken from a charity's accounts that complied, is as follows:

Example 11.1

THE ROYAL SOCIETY

Summary Income and Expenditure Account for the year ended 31 March 1996

	£'000	£'000
	1996	1995
Continuing operations:		
Gross income from all sources	9,154	8,486
Expenditure	7,888	8,564
Net income/(expenditure) for the year		
before investment asset disposals	1,266	(78)
Gain on disposal of investments	401	1,459
Net income for the year	1,667	1,381

The Summary Income and Expenditure Account is derived from the Statement of Financial Activities on page G6. Detailed analyses of the income and expenditure are provided in the Statement of Financial Activities and Notes 1 and 2 respectively.

Certain charities have ignored the 1995 SORP requirement to produce a summary income and expenditure account where in their view the movement was not material. For example, the Mental Health Foundation did not produce a separate summary income and expenditure account although its consolidated SOFA for the year ended 31 March 1996 showed unrealised gains of £405. As this was the only movement on endowment funds where the balances at the beginning of the year had been £240,675, they felt the amount was not material and said so in their accounting policies. To quote:

> 'A separate summary income and expenditure account has not been prepared as required by the Companies Act 1985 because the movement on capital funds as shown in the statement of financial activities is not material.'

Checklist for a summary income and expenditure account

		SORP (paragraph)
1	Does this summary have to be prepared?	Paras 22(b), 24 & 335
2	Is this account derived from, and cross-referenced to, the corresponding figures in the SOFA?	Para. 337
3	Has the following information been given:	Para. 337
	i Gross income from all sources,	
	ii Net gains/losses from disposals of all fixed assets belonging to the charity's income funds?	
	iii Transfers from endowment funds of capital resources converted into income?	
	iv Total income?	
	v Total expenditure?	
	vi Net income or expenditure for the year?	

Balance sheet

If a columnar format is chosen then charitable companies will still have to show the funds of the charity as a single line or split between the various different types of fund in order to comply with the Companies Act requirements (SORP, paragraph 339). Where fixed assets have been revalued upwards a revaluation reserve will arise being the difference between the original depreciated cost or valuation of the asset and the revalued amount. Separate reporting of the reserve is not significant for charities as they do not distribute profits.

However the revaluation reserve that will nevertheless arise will form part of the funds in which the revalued assets are held. In certain circumstances, as set out in FRSS 11 and 15, impairment losses or other downward revaluations can be offset against the revaluation reserves (SORP, paragraph 340).

To comply with the Companies Act 1985 charitable companies must separately disclose the revaluation reserve within the fund section on the face of the balance sheet but may change the heading as appropriate (SORP, paragraph 341).

Summary financial information

As we have already seen (chapter 9) charitable companies must comply with the rules laid down by the Companies Act but should also follow the recommendations set out in the SORP for summary financial information (SORP, paragraphs 292–7). Any summary financial information prepared by a charitable company will almost all be non-statutory and the auditor's report cannot be published with them without the statutory accounts to which it relates. This means that in effect that the companies can produce summarised accounts without the backing of an audit report (SORP, paragraphs 342 and 343).

12 Accounting for Smaller Charities

Introduction

In the context of the SORP a smaller charity is one that, due to its size, does not have to adopt all the requirements of the revised SORP (SORP, paragraph 344). A charity which is under the threshold for small companies, as described in the Companies Acts, can follow the Financial Reporting Standard For Smaller Entities (FRSSE) in preparing its financial accounts, except where those conflict with the revised SORP (SORP, paragraph 345). However, in following the FRSSE the accounts will meet most of the requirements of the revised SORP for such entities. The SOFA replaces the profit and loss account and the principles of fund accounting will have to be adopted throughout the accounts (SORP, paragraph 346).

Additionally, all investments, including investment properties, must be shown at market value; foreign exchange gains and losses, which may be allowed to be taken to reserves in the FRSSE, must be shown in the bottom section of the SOFA; and exceptional items. which are required to be shown after operating profit, must be shown in an appropriate place in the SOFA (SORP, paragraph 347).

Charities with a gross income not exceeding £250,000 preparing accounts on the accruals basis do not have to use the expenditure headings and sub-headings as set out in the SORP, paragraph 60. Alternatively, they may choose expenditure classifications to suit their own circumstances, for example, salaries and wages, office costs, repairs and maintenance, etc. (SORP, paragraph 348).

Non-company charities in England and Wales that prepare accounts on the accruals basis are required to make disclosures of particulars of any material departure from the recommendations in the revised SORP in accordance with paragraph 280. A departure is not justified simply because it gives the reader a more appealing picture of the financial position or results of the charity (SORP, paragraph 349).

Definition of a smaller charity

A smaller charity is defined for this purpose as one with an annual gross income of less than £100,000. In particular, we have seen the introduction of what is described as the 'light touch' regime for charities whose gross income and total expenditure does not exceed £10,000. In cases of charities whose gross income does not exceed £1,000 and which have neither a permanent endowment nor use or occupy land, these charities are not required to register, but they must maintain proper accounting records, prepare accounts and make those accounts available to the public on request.

Many smaller charities are managed, and services provided, internally by volunteers. Quite frequently there are no professional resources available and if they are, they are insufficient to meet all their requirements. Many have taken the view that the SORP as revised would place a considerably onerous burden upon the smaller charity for this reason. Fortunately, as we have seen earlier (Chapter 2), the thresholds laid down in the Charities Act 1993 were changed so that the burden will now be far less than was originally feared.

It is very important that a proper balance is found between the requirements for supervision and the need to reduce, if not remove entirely, all the burdens of accounting for a charity. Charity trustees have been afforded a certain degree of flexibility regarding the preparation of receipts and payments accounts and considerable guidance is available, including much from the Charity Commission themselves.

Definition – problems

Before looking at some of the possible effects of the regulations and the recommendations on the smaller charity registered in England and Wales, it will be appropriate to start with a definition of what is meant by 'smaller'.

For accounting purposes, a charity will be 'smaller' if it does not exceed one or more of certain thresholds of gross income and for certain purposes total expenditure for the year. However, for certain purposes of the Charities Act 1993 the definition is different again, for example up to £5,000 gross income a registered charity is not required by section 5 of the Act to declare its registered status on appeals literature, checks, receipts, purchase orders, sales invoices, etc.

The table below sets out the reliefs/options that are available to the smaller charity under the regulations.

INCOME NOT EXCEEDING £	EXPENDITURE NOT EXCEEDING £	RELIEF OR OPTION
1,000	–	Need not prepare annual report unless registered (registration is legally binding if the charity has an endowment or the use or occupation of land); can opt to prepare accounts on the receipts and payments basis or need not note in accruals accounts any departure from accounting standards and the SORP and need not follow standard expenditure heading in the SOFA; and not required by law to have independent examination or audit of the accounts.
10,000	10,000	Can prepare abbreviated form of annual report and omit any reference to how the charity is organised and to assets held as custodian trustee; can opt to prepare accounts on a receipts and payments basis or need not note in accruals accounts any departure from accounting standards and the SORP and need not follow standard expenditure headings in the SOFA; not required by law to have independent examination or audit of the accounts; not required routinely to file annual report and accounts with the Charity Commission; and not required to file annual return for monitoring purposes – only for updating the Charity Commission's public register information.
100,000	–	Can prepare abbreviated form of annual report; and can opt to prepare accounts on the receipts and payments basis or need not note in accruals accounts any departure from accounting standards and the sorp and need not follow standard expenditure headings in the SOFA.

It must be noted that, even if not smaller, any charity that has been set up in respect of a registered place of public worship or which belongs to the class of excepted charities is not legally obliged to register with the Charity Commission and, unless it voluntarily registers, it will not have to file a copy of its annual report with the Charity Commission unless specifically asked to do so.

However, in the Charity Commission's report for 2000 they make the following point:

> 'The original decisions on the policy behind voluntary registration were taken in the early 1960s. The purpose of registration is now changed, with the introduction of monitoring under the Charities Act 1993. Some of the current rules on voluntary registration expire next year. As matters stand about 25,000 religious charities will then have to register. The Commission and the Home Office have recently consulted on the future basis of voluntary registration.'

(This Charity Commission report was issued during 2000 so that the reference to 'next year' effectively means 2001.)

Charity Commission statistics

The Charity Commission's definition of smaller means that approximately 143,000 charities (90 per cent of the total) are regarded in this way and will not have to comply with the full rigours of the regulations or the SORP. This is because they are being specifically exempted.

What is the true size of the charity sector in England and Wales? Not an easy question to answer, but for those charities registered with the Charity Commission which have to produce accounts, the following table makes interesting reading. The table is based on information provided by the Charity Commission of the number of registered charities in England and Wales in 1999 that are not associated with other charities.

The Charity Commission's Report for 2000 in discussing the issue of the size of the charity sector makes the point that:

> 'The pattern has remained consistent with the previous year, showing that although concentration of numbers is in the lower income bands, the concentration of income is in a relatively few very large charities.'

RANGE	NUMBER OF CHARITIES WITHIN RANGE	PERCENTAGE OF TOTAL
Gross income of less than £10,000	106,000	67
Gross income of over £10,000 but less than £100,000	37,000	23
Gross income of over £100,000 but less than £250,000	8,000	5
Gross income of over £250,000	8,000	5
Total	159,000	

The Commission's financial monitoring concentrates on the one third of charities with gross income above £10,000 a year, and special attention is paid to the 10 per cent with income above £100,000.

'Light touch' regime

The Charity Commission definition of smaller means that many charities are regarded in this way and do not have to comply with the full rigours of the regulations or the SORP. This is because they are being specifically exempted. Indeed, many escape almost entirely thanks to what is described as the 'light touch' regime.

Charities with a gross income of less than £10,000 (67 per cent of the total and equal to about 106,000 charities) do not have to file copies of their accounts with the Charity Commission, do not need to have those accounts reviewed by an independent third party and may produce a receipts and payments set of accounts if they wish. In addition, charities with an annual income of less than £1,000 which do not have a permanent endowment do not need to register with the Charity Commission.

However, all registered charities, regardless of size, have to submit an annual return. For the smaller charity this is a fairly simplified one. Any charity can, of course, choose to impose upon itself more rigorous rules than those laid down. For example, a charity with an income of less than £100,000 can, if it wants, elect to produce accrual accounts. Of course, if the charity is incorporated then it must produce accounts prepared on the accruals basis.

Smaller charities, as a legal minimum, are subject to independent examination rather than audit, unless their annual gross income is less than £10,000, in which case they do not need to be reviewed at all. Independent examination (see further Chapter 13) is a less onerous form of scrutiny than audit, both in terms of the depth of work and the qualification of the individual who carries out the work.

Whilst the revised SORP and the regulations call for a considerable amount of detail to be shown in the annual report, those for the smaller charity need only be a brief summary of the main activities and achievements of the charity during the year in relation to its objects.

Receipts and payments

For the small charity (defined for these purposes as those with a gross income or total expenditure for any one year of less than £100,000) accounts may be produced on a receipts and payments basis, provided that the small charity is not a limited company. Care should also be paid to the governing document as to its instructions relating to the preparation of accounts (SORP, paragraphs 350 and 352). The Charity Commission has published useful guidance in the form of booklet CC64 SORP 2000: Receipts and Payments Accounts Pack.

Accounts

Charities with gross income below the threshold set by Ministerial Order (currently £100,000) may choose between producing accrual accounts or receipts and payments accounts, as set out in Part VI of the Charities Act 1993, which regulates the form and content of the accounts of most charities in England and Wales. There are similar alternatives for Scottish charities in line with regulations following the Law Reform (Miscellaneous Provisions) (Scotland) Act 1990. However, small charitable companies must always prepare accrual accounts and are not covered by these concessions.

Accounts prepared on the receipts and payments basis constitute only a factual record summarising the small charity's cash transactions and listing its remaining cash and non-cash assets and its liabilities, and do not purport to show a true and fair view of the small charity's financial activities and state of affairs. Accounting standards, which are primarily concerned with the presentation of a true and fair view, will therefore not generally apply to such accounts. The only fundamental accounting concept that has to be applied will be consistency of accounting treatment. In other words, the way in which the accounts are produced each year should be consistent with the year before. The accruals concept will not apply; nor will there be a need for prudence or 'the going concern basis concepts to be used'.

The 1995 SORP recommended the introduction of what it describes as 'functional classification for reporting of costs', that is to show in the SOFA what has been expended on charitable objectives, publicity and fundraising, and management and administration costs. The regulations make it clear that small charities who have not opted to use accrual accounting as the basis for reporting their figures will not have to provide a functional classification split of costs. In other words, the receipts and payments account continues to show expenditure on the natural classification basis, for example salaries, wages, and so on.

A statement of assets and liabilities is needed. This is a list of the cash and non-cash assets and liabilities of the small charity as at the period end date of the receipts and payments account. However, there is no need to list all individual assets but the list must be comprehensive in covering all classes of asset held by the small charity trustees. Values are not required unless it is deemed to be essential to a meaningful description of the asset, for example, cash and other monetary assets. As in all cases, throughout the SORP trustees may go further than the basic requirements and therefore show valuations for these assets and liabilities but if they do so must follow the rules shown in the SORP in relation to accrual accounts.

Notes to the accounts

For the small charity which is preparing accounts on the receipts and payments basis there will effectively be no need to produce any notes to the accounts as required by the revised SORP. However, where the small charity opts to prepare accrual accounts, it will have to comply with the regulations and follow the SORP in producing notes to the accounts.

Special aspects

The SOFA in the accounts of a small unendowed charity which holds no funds on 'special trust' (that is, which must be spent on specified purposes

– restricted) and has no fixed asset revaluation gains/losses looks no different from the old income and expenditure account except for the addition of brought forward and carried forward fund balances. Receipts and payments accounts for the small charity post the SORP are also very little different in their format from those pre the SORP.

One major change, however, was that as a result of section 47 of the Charities Act 1993 the trustees must, within two months of any written request and subject to payment of any reasonable copying fee they may require, provide any member of the public who makes the request with a copy of the most recent accounts prepared.

Endowments and special trusts administered as part of the small charity should be accounted for in such a way that it can be seen from the accounts that the terms of trust are being complied with. Branches or local groups controlled by the small charity and which raise funds in the name of the small charity on its behalf need to be accounted for by inclusion in the small charity's accounts.

Non-monetary benefits provided to a small charity will present accounting problems. They cannot be shown in receipts and payments accounts but have to be when accrual accounting is carried out. However, assets, such as property, which have been received as a gift for the benefit of the small charity should appear in the year end statement of assets and liabilities where receipts and payments accounts are produced. All tangible benefits that the charity receives or provides should in any case be suitably described in the annual report in a way that will indicate their value and importance to the small charity.

Where the small charity carries out charitable trading either through the charity or through a trading subsidiary then information on this should be shown separately in the accounts.

Change in accounting basis

Where because of size or decision of the trustees the small charity changes from producing its accounts on a receipts and payments basis to full accrual accounting (or vice versa) the corresponding amounts for the previous financial years should be restated on the basis of the new accounting policy (SORP, paragraph 357).

Independent examination

Where receipts and payments accounts are subject to external examination this will normally be done by an independent examiner. However,
the Charities Auditing Practice Note 11 (APN 11) does allow for the audit
of receipts and payments accounts by a registered auditor, although of
course a 'true and fair' opinion cannot be given. Therefore an audit
provision does not demand the production of accruals accounts.
Additionally, there may be a requirement, for example by the governing
instrument or by a donor, for both an audit by a registered auditor and
for accrual accounts to be prepared.

Although this independent examination is a less onerous form of
scrutiny and is to be welcomed by charities, they should be aware that
many of them, because of their own constitution/trust deed, etc., will
require audit whatever their size. Also, many funders, particularly local
authorities, will demand of the charity to whom it is making grants that
audited accounts are supplied. This is a problem that trustees will have to
resolve if they want to make use of the new independent examination
procedures.

Finally, there are different rules for charitable companies. In certain
cases this requires a lower standard of scrutiny than for the unincorporated charity! Currently, incorporated charities with an income of
less than £90,000 do not require any review at all whilst of course
unincorporated charities with this level of income, provided it is in excess
of £10,000, will require an independent examination.

See further Chapter 13.

Accruals

The concept of accruals, which is one of the four fundamental accounting
concepts, means that, for the purpose of charities, the incoming resources
or funds and the expenditure of those resources or funds are accrued.
That is that the income is recognised when earned as in the case of
revenue or when receivable as in the case of gifts, donations, bequests,
grants etc. and for expenditure when it is incurred not as for receipts of
payments when money is received or paid.

The accruals basis of accounting matches activities and their income
against the costs incurred so that both are usually included within the

same accounting period, using prudent estimates where necessary. It would be prudent, for example, to take credit for contract income without a corresponding accrual in the accounts to cover any further costs expected to be incurred in completing the contract.

To give another example, if from one year's revenue a charity purchases all its stationery on a bulk discount order to cover the next three years then the accounting treatment will be different for receipts and payments and an accruals basis. For simple receipts and payments accounts the absence of stationery costs in years 2 and 3 might not be at all obvious from studying the year's accounts. The uninformed reader may even think that the charity does not require any stationery.

Under the accruals method the stationery costs will be apportioned to each year, by regarding the cost of any substantial year end stocks as probably either a prepayment of stationery for future use to match them with the activities of that year or as stock in hand. Therefore, the accounts would in any year be adjusted to show the required true and fair view picture of the charity's financial activities and position.

Thus one introduces the idea of debtors and creditors. As an example where a Gift Aid payment has been received from an individual and the tax repayment applied for but not received by the year-end it would under accrual accounting be accrued for. Thus if the payment was a net £78 with tax to be recovered at £22 under accrual accounting the figure shown in the accounts in the year would be £100 whilst, at least in the first year, under receipts and payments basis it would just be £78.

This accrual concept therefore matches income with expenditure so far as their relationship can be established or justifiably assumed and deals with it accordingly in the SOFA of the period to which it relates. However, this is provided that the accruals concept is not inconsistent with the prudence concept, in which case the latter will prevail.

The accruals concept implies that the SOFA reflects changes in the amount of net assets that arise out of the transactions and events of the relevant period. Incoming resources or funds dealt with in the SOFA are matched with associated costs and expenses by including in the same account the costs incurred or to be incurred in earning the revenues or in receiving the gifts, donations, bequests or grants (so far as these costs are material and identifiable).

With accrual accounting one will therefore have a balance sheet and the purchase of fixed assets will go to the balance sheet and be written off over a period of time. Hence we have the charge of depreciation in the SOFA when it is produced on an accruals basis which will not apply when the SOFA is produced on a receipts and payments basis.

The Charity Commission has published very useful guidance notes CC65 SORP 2000: Accrual Accounts Pack.

13 Audit and Independent Examination

Introduction

Charity audit is an audit of stewardship and there is a considerable overlap between the role of the external auditor and the charity finance director.

There is no such thing as a private charity – secrecy is out and a greater openness is required. All those involved in a charity – the stakeholders – whether they are donors, recipients, trustees or employees, have the right to expect that the resources entrusted to the charity are being used cost-effectively. It must, therefore, be part of the audit to ensure that this happens.

The decision on whether a charity needs audit or independent examination depends on its size. To meet the requirements of the Charities Act 1993 all charities with an income in excess of £250,000 require audit. Incorporated charities with income up to £90,000 do not require audit and those with income within the range £90,000 to £250,000 are entitled to an audit exemption report.

The charity audit – some important aspects

Requirements

Until the Charities Act 1993 there was no statutory auditing requirement for charities. The Charity Commissioners did, however, have power under section 8 (3) of the Charities Act 1960 to:

> 'Require that the condition and accounts of a charity for such period as they think fit shall be investigated and audited by an auditor appointed by them.'

Section 22 (4) of the Trustee Act 1925 empowers trustees:

> 'In their absolute discretion, from time to time, but not more than once in every three years unless the nature of the trust or any special dealings with the trust property make a more frequent exercise of the right reasonable, cause the accounts of the trust property to be examined or audited by an independent accountant.'

In addition, certain charities may have to have an audit. For example:

- those incorporated under the Companies Acts;
- those incorporated under the Industrial and Provident Societies Acts;
- charitable housing associations;
- war charities or charities for disabled, governed by the War Charities Act 1940;
- charitable friendly societies.

Both the Woodfield Report (1987) and the White Paper 'Charities a Framework for the Future' (1989) proposed forms of audit or examination according to the size of charities. There followed a Bill debated in the House of Lords towards the end of 1991 from which emerged the Charities Act 1992, now mainly consolidated into the 1993 Act.

The audit requirements of the Act set out that if a charity's gross income or total expenditure in any of the following:

a relevant year;

b financial year of the charity immediately preceding the relevant year; and

c financial year of the charity immediately preceding the year specified in paragraph (b);

exceed £250,000 then the accounts will have to be audited by a person who:

i is in accordance with Section 25 of the Companies Act 1989 eligible for appointment as a company auditor; or

ii is a member of a body for the time being specified in the regulations still to be laid out and is under the rules of that body eligible for appointment as auditor of the charity.

Where the annual gross income or total expenditure is less than £250,000 but more than £10,000 in any of the specified years the accounts have to be independently examined by a person who, in the opinion of the trustees, is reasonably believed to have the requisite ability and practical experience to carry out a competent examination of the accounts. (See below, p. 144.) Alternatively, they can if they wish have the accounts audited.

The need to be eligible as a company auditor implies that the same considerations of independence apply. Statutory Instrument 2000 No. 1430: Audit Exemption came into force on 26 May 2000 and applies to accounting periods ending on or after 26 July 2000. As a result of this, audit exemption for charitable companies remains unchanged with full exemption for charitable companies with gross income under £90,000 and an audit exemption report required for those with gross income of between £90,000 and £250,000 (see further Chapter 2). Ethical guidance is also relevant. Charity audit is at a higher risk than other audits due to the level of public interest and often media interest in charity accounts.

Some overall considerations

Charities exist not to generate profits but to meet an identified charitable objective. Financial performance is not, therefore, measured merely by surplus or deficit, and the success and operational performance of a charity are measured differently from those of a commercial organisation. The primary purpose of the charity is paramount. Accounting systems, therefore, must reflect the activities of the charity and provide sufficient information to control and manage those activities.

Accounting by charities is reflected in the revised SORP and not primarily driven by FRSs/SSAPs. Therefore, in considering the appropriateness of these financial reporting standards it must be remembered that they have been prepared to deal with business enterprises where the motive is profit. Charities' motive is certainly different. What is a true and fair view for a non-profit organisation may not be so for a profit-oriented organisation.

Audit scope

The scope of the audit may depend on the status of the charity. This will also determine the type of any report that has to be given. It is essential that any auditor or independent examiner should know and understand the legal structure of the organisation and recognise what is included within the audit scope.

Charities are governed in many different ways:
- as a company probably limited by guarantee;
- as a Trust;
- as an unincorporated association;
- by Royal Charter;
- by a specific Act of Parliament; or
- under one of the various acts relating to friendly, industrial and provident societies and housing associations.

The purpose of an audit must be to provide independent confirmation of the financial affairs of an organisation. Therefore, the terms of the auditors' appointment should determine the actual scope of the audit and the nature of the report required. The requirements of a charity audit became clearer following the publication of the accounting regulations and in 1996 the Auditing Practices Board guidance Practice Note 11, *The Audit of Charities* (currently being reviewed and revised).

As we have seen in business operations, the auditors will be required to express the opinion that the accounts give a 'true and fair' view. This concept has been debated, often hotly, in many forums and there continues to be an expectation gap between what the trustees or the staff of the charity think they are receiving from the audit and what the auditor thinks is being provided. Therefore, it is vital that the scope of the audit is clearly defined in the letter of engagement, which it is important that the auditors are willing to discuss with the client.

As well as commentating on the accounts, the auditors should also review the trustees' report. The production of such a report is a legal requirement and it is therefore necessary to ensure that the information in this report is consistent with that given in the financial statements. As many in the charity world are prone to exaggeration, this can sometimes lead to problems.

What the audit should provide

The charity should get more from the audit than just a management letter; it is essential that the auditors are seen as part of the team. There certainly must not be an attempt by the auditors to 'hijack' the accounts, which are those of the charity. Independence has to be maintained, but empathy is important. So from the point of view of the charity, what should the audit provide? As a basic minimum:

- independent review;
- value for money;
- more than just a checking of the figures;
- innovative ideas;
- practical advice.

Not surprisingly, little of the training a chartered accountant receives seems to involve any understanding of how a business works, let alone how a charity does. Certainly, there is nothing on charity and trust law.

To be truly effective therefore it is important that the charity audit team specialises and gains this experience by repeated involvement. However, it would be quite wrong for any charity to bear the cost of this learning curve and quite clearly there is a need for further detailed charity audit and accounting training.

Like many organisations, the annual report and accounts are used by a charity as part of its PR and it is therefore important that the auditor provides advice on presentation.

Fundamentals of an effective audit

The specific guidelines on charity audits were originally published on 22 October 1996. The guidelines, issued as Practice Note 11, *The Audit of Charities*, take the form of commentary on factors to be considered by auditors in order to meet the requirements of the Auditing Practices Board's Auditing Standards when undertaking the audit of a charity's financial statements. It also provides background information on the regulatory and legal framework relating to charities in the United Kingdom. At the time of writing (May 2001) the APB is reviewing the Practice Note in light of the revised SORP, the Regulations and its own operating effectiveness. An exposure draft is due out shortly.

Besides its relevance to auditors, the Practice Note contains much that would be of interest to trustees and others involved in the management of charities, and should help them to gain a better understanding of both the auditors' work and the way in which charities can benefit from the audit process. The application of auditing standards is no different in the case of charities from the case of other organisations.

The Practice Note sets out special considerations relating to the audit of charities which arise from individual Statements of Auditing Standards (SAS). Where no special considerations apply no comment is made. The following SASs are included:

SAS 110: Fraud and error.

SAS 120: Consideration of law and regulations.

SAS 130: The going concern basis in financial statements.

SAS 140: Engagement letters.

SAS 160: Other information in documents containing audited financial statements.

SAS 210: Knowledge of the business.

SAS 220: Materiality and the audit.

SAS 300: Accounting and internal control systems and audit risk assessments.

SAS 400: Audit evidence.

SAS 410: Analytical procedures.

SAS 420: Audit of accounting estimates.

SAS 440: Management representations.

SAS 450: Opening balances and comparatives.

SAS 460: Related parties.

SAS 470: Overall review of financial statements.

SAS 510: The relationship between principal auditors and other auditors.

SAS 600: Auditors' reports on financial statements.

SAS 610: Reports to directors or management.

SAS 620: The auditors' right and duty to report to regulators in the financial sector.

The purpose of this Practice Note is to provide guidance on the application of auditing standards when auditing a charity, rather than a general commentary on such audits. The approach taken has therefore been to consider the various SASs issued by the APB and to provide guidance on matters specific to the audit of a charity's financial statements. There is, therefore, an attempt to incorporate, within this framework, all the major issues that are likely to need particular application of judgement by auditors. More specifically, the five key areas covered are:

- factors affecting auditors' assessment of risk;
- analysis of relevant law and regulations;
- controls over key aspects of a charity's income and assets;
- matters to be reported directly to the Charity Commission; and
- content of report on financial statements.

The fundamentals of an effective audit should be to:

- understand the activity;
- identify key areas;
- assess risk;
- plan;
- monitor progress;
- report.

It is vital that the auditor knows the organisation and understands fully what its mandate and mission are. The auditor should know where the money comes from, where it is going and the systems within the organisation for controlling income, expenditure, staff resources, etc.

The starting point is to identify those key areas within which the charity operates both in its fundraising and operating field. Some of these have considerably more risk than others and it is here that concentration on the sensitive areas is essential. Charities are forever changing the way in which they fundraise as new innovative ideas come forward. As a result, the business will change, often dramatically, from year to year. It is important that audits should be planned and structured in a way that takes account of this, but also assist the management of the charity in the task of both maximising the resources available and ensuring that they are applied to achieve the charitable objectives as cost-effectively as possible. Monitoring progress then becomes vital. One of the complaints frequently heard from charity finance directors is that they never know what is happening whilst the audit is in progress, and worse still, the reports at the end of the charity audit seem to take far too long to arrive.

Auditing income

There are as many types of charity – probably more – than there are types of business. Charity is not just one industry but many complex ones. The main difference in audit approach has to be due to the nature of voluntary income, which is so different from the turnover of a 'normal' for-profit enterprise as to make it extremely difficult to audit. There will not be a sales invoice for a donation, although of course there should or could be a receipt. Quite clearly, in the case of legacy income, despatch notes and invoices will be unheard of; however, there should be an audit trail via a chain of letters to and from the executors of the legacy. Only when a charity goes into trading activity are there likely to be any profit margins.

Much – probably most – of the income of a fundraising charity will be unsolicited and this leads to considerable difficulties in verification of completeness. It will be quite easy to audit what is there, but very difficult to confirm that it is all there. However, attempts must be made to do this. It is extremely important for the auditor to ascertain in relation to income:

- What was its origin?
- What restrictions, if any exist, on its use?
- What is its nature?

Why are these questions important? Consideration of these three questions in particular should, in the case of the origin, allow judgements to be made about whether it is all there and how to audit it. For example, in the case of legacy income, which forms over 60 per cent of the income of the Cancer Research Campaign, one needs to look at whether it is a pecuniary legacy, a specific bequest or part of the residue. Have there been any interim payments? Have inheritance tax and capital gains tax implications been taken care of? Here it should be a fairly straight-forward process to audit the correspondence between the charity staff and the executors of the will and, where necessary, examine the wills concerned.

Second, any money received in trust must be used for the purpose for which it was given. The restriction principle is paramount and any unspent restricted income has to be carried forward and separately identified in the accounts. The use of restricted funds is very tightly controlled and needs to be easily identifiable in the accounts. Paperwork supporting legacy income should be reviewed to ensure that the terms of the will do not stipulate the setting-up of a restricted fund with a specific purpose.

Recognition of the nature of the income is vital. Charities are governed by strict rules in what they can and cannot do. Contrary to popular misbelief there are many tax implications for charities – for example, the raising of funds is in itself not a charitable objective and consequently trading is usually outside the scope of activities that can be carried on by a charity. Thus if it has carried out this business within the charity it is essential that this is looked at in considerable detail.

Grants should not be recognised until the conditions for receipt have been met. If there is a likelihood of the grant having to be repaid, it should be treated as a contingent liability. Grants restricted to future accounting periods should be deferred and recognised in the future accounting period to which it relates, and the basis for apportionment should be explained in the notes to the accounts. Grants for immediate financial support and assistance should be recognised immediately in the SOFA. A description of the sources of material grants, by category, should be disclosed in the accounts. (By category refers to whether the grant is, for example, from a local authority or government department.)

The possibility of there being gifts in kind or intangible income will need to be reviewed with the client. A valuation will need to be established where the gift is capable of measurement. If material, the gift should be disclosed by way of a note and an accounting policy showing the basis of valuation incorporated. Some other possible examples of evidence that can be reviewed to verify the figures in the books are:

- published literature;
- minutes of meetings – particularly fundraising committees;
- membership records – where applicable;
- comparison of events income with entrance fees, etc.;
- Gift Aid records;
- internal notice boards;
- correspondence from donors;
- comparison of raffle/lottery proceeds with details of tickets sold (e.g. stubs);
- attendance at occasional functions.

Auditing expenditure

This is somewhat more straightforward. Generally, the audit of expenditure is a control over the purchases, payments and creditor cycle. Additionally, with a charity it is important that a check is made to ensure that payments are within its charitable objective purposes. The audit approach should therefore check the adequacy of controls over:

- analysis;
- allocation and matching with income;
- ordering procedures;
- creditors records;
- commitments;
- value for money.

For restricted funds it is necessary to ensure correct use of the income for the purposes intended. Endowment funds need to be very carefully scrutinised. Under trustee law the trustees of a charity or trustees' family or business connections are not allowed to benefit from their involvement in the charity in any way. This includes remuneration, beneficial loans, gifts or services. Any such benefit must be disclosed in the accounts by reference to the source, the recipient and the amount. Exceptions to this are where the constitution permits it. The fact that the trustees have received no remuneration must be stated in the accounts.

Many charities pay their trustees' expenses in respect of their attendance at meetings. Under the SORP the number of trustees in receipt of expenses should be disclosed, together with the total of the expenses and an indication of what the expenses are for. In most cases this will be for travel and subsistence. If the trustees have received no reimbursement that fact must be stated.

Trustees are liable for the consequences of the charity if it can be proved they acted in breach of trust. The Charity Commission is able to take proceedings in court to recover from the trustees personally. In order to guard against this, insurance cover is available under which trustees can insure themselves against such a claim. In the instances of such insurance being taken out the fact that the insurance has been purchased, why and the costs incurred need to be disclosed in the accounts.

The normal payroll work undertaken in the course of an audit will need to be done. However, in addition to this the number of employees whose emoluments were in excess of £50,000 needs to be disclosed in the accounts. The banding by which this is shown is different from the old Companies Act requirement, as the banding of the remuneration is £10,000 and not £5,000. If no employees received remuneration in excess of £50,000 this fact needs to be stated.

Some charities make material payments of grants. Where this is the case the name of the recipient institution and the aggregate amount of the grant made to that recipient in the accounting period needs to be shown. The definition of material depends on the size of the charity. If the proportion of expenditure spent on grants is less than 5 per cent, no disclosure needs to be made. Where disclosure is required all grants made over £1,000 in this instance should be disclosed. In the case of a large grant making organisation this can be restricted to the largest fifty grants.

If the trustees consider the disclosure of this information to be detrimental to the charity or the recipient, this information may be withheld but the full amount of all the grants made should be disclosed. In cases of grants made to individuals, only the aggregate value and the number of grants need be disclosed.

Audit evidence

The auditor should give special attention to the possibility of:
- understatement or incompleteness of the records of income;
- overstatement of expenses, in particular cash grants;

- misanalysis or misuse in the application of funds;
- misstatement or omission of assets;
- the existence of restricted or uncontrollable funds in foreign or independent branches.

Internal controls

Large charities will – or rather should – have internal controls appropriate to any large enterprise, and the auditors should look for and encourage the charity to implement internal controls and reporting systems in keeping with the scale of operations. In considering internal controls, the auditor should bear in mind any related reporting requirements. For example, the Friendly Societies Act 1992 requires that the audit report has a statement to the effect that a satisfactory system of control over transactions has (or has not) been maintained. Obviously the smaller the charity the weaker are likely to be the internal controls. Here the use of volunteers and trustees in ensuring that all procedures have been correctly followed is advised.

Review of financial statements

As normal the auditor should consider whether the accounting policies adopted are appropriate to the specific objectives, activities and constitution of the charity. In particular the auditor should consider the basis of:
- disclosing income from fundraising activities (i.e. net or gross);
- accounting for income and expenditure (accrual or cash basis);
- the capitalising of expenditure on fixed assets;
- apportioning overhead expenditure;
- accounting for income from donations and legacies;
- considering the possible exposure to taxation.

Going concern

Charities without significant endowment or accumulated funds will often be dependent upon future income from voluntary sources in order to meet the financial commitments arising from the continuation of their activities. Thus the review of the financial statements may lead the auditor to question whether a going concern basis of accounting is appropriate. However, before forming a conclusion on the matter, the auditor should take account of the amount of, and trends in, income and expenditure since the accounting date, any forecast and representations by management as to future income and expenditure and (where relevant) the market value of the charity's tangible assets.

Statutory reports

There is no common report possible for all charities because they have different constitutions and will be governed by many differing rules and laws. For example, the auditor's report on the financial statements of a charity registered under the Companies Act will continue to be determined in accordance with the provisions of that Act and addressed to the members of the charity. However the auditor's report on the financial statements of a charity registered under the Acts relating to friendly, industrial and provident societies will be in a different form and addressed to the charity itself. Whilst on this topic, one particular complaint from charities relates to a paragraph which used to occur far too frequently in audit reports. This ran along the lines of:

> 'This charity derives a substantial proportion of its income from voluntary donations which is not susceptible to independent audit verification until entered in the main accounting records.'

This gave many the wrong impression that the accounts were being qualified and implied that something was wrong when most frequently it was not. Fortunately, this sort of comment is now slowly disappearing. Although there can be a particular and frequent problem for many small charities in the difficulty of applying proper control over voluntary donations, until they are received this is something which is inherent throughout the charity world. Auditors should, therefore, consider very carefully when reviewing the accounts what they put in their reports.

In these cases, provided the auditor is satisfied that the system of accounting and control is reasonable having regard to the size and nature of the charities operation, then there is no reason for such a statement to be inserted into the audit report or for the accounts to be qualified. As the APB Practice Note 11 puts it when commenting on SAS 400:

> 'Whilst it is the trustees' responsibility to safeguard the assets and income of the charity, the voluntary nature of some elements of its income raises considerations concerning the methods available to the trustees for the purpose of ensuring that all income to which the

charity is entitled is correctly accounted for. These considerations differ from those in commercial concerns: the amount of voluntary donations cannot be determined in advance, nor can a charity be regarded as necessarily entitled to funds, even when the amounts can be predicted, before they are donated. Trustees of a charity cannot be held responsible for the security of money or other assets that are intended for its use until that money or assets are within the control of the charity.'

The last sentence is particularly important, and must be borne in mind by *all* auditors of charities. The APB Practice Note goes on to say:

'When considering whether the donated income of a charity is properly recorded, therefore, auditors seek evidence to determine whether the accounting records reflect cash and other forms of donation and the point at which the charity is entitled to them. Where the auditors are satisfied, through valuation and testing, that there are appropriate and effective controls, they can use the results of their internal control testing as a source of audit evidence about the completeness of reported transactions.'

It is to be hoped that auditors of charities are following the Practice Note's guidance in relation to this important point and not qualifying the accounts for what are really spurious commercial reasons.

Audit management report

These are still not used as frequently in the charity world as elsewhere and it is vitally important that they are, so that the charity can derive full benefit from them. The report should not simply be a catalogue of what is wrong and it should certainly not be destructive criticism. What it should be is helpful, pointing out any weaknesses and providing ways of overcoming them, whilst at the same time suggesting ideas for building on the strengths.

The report should report on the standard of the accounts and the systems on which they are based, paying particular attention to controls in existence. The charity's attention should be drawn to departures from best practice within the charity sector and from the law. Any known changes, – for example, revised Charities SORP – should be highlighted for the benefit of the charity client. Often these arrive late, are produced well after the accounts have been signed off, and quite frequently so far into the following year as to be useless as a tool for planning improvements.

In summary

Both the management of the charity and the auditors should recognise and expect that the auditors can and should do more than just provide an audit report. Relationships with the charity – and certainly with the larger charities – will frequently be with the executive management. It is essential that the auditors also meet the trustees or at least those who have financial responsibility. The Charities Act effectively came about because of the increasing demand from the public that charities be properly controlled and efficiently managed. It is therefore essential that auditors should contribute to this.

Independent examination

Whether or not independent examination is required for a smaller charity depends on the legal status of the charity. Unincorporated charities with income of £250,000 or less can have an independent examination unless their constitution specifically requires an audit.

What is an independent examination?

It is a less onerous form of scrutiny than audit, both in terms of the depth of work that is to be carried out and the qualification necessary to undertake such work. It does not lead to the expression of an opinion that the accounts show a true and fair view. Instead, it highlights whether certain matters have been brought to the reviewer's attention. The work must include the following procedures:

- obtaining an understanding of the activities and structure of the charity to plan appropriate examination procedures;
- checking that the election for independent examination is valid;
- recording the procedures carried out and the conclusions reached;
- comparing the accounts with the accounting records to ensure they are in accordance with one another;
- reviewing the accounting records to identify gross failures to maintain proper records;
- carrying out analytical review to identify unusual items or disclosures in the accounts, obtaining explanations and, if necessary, obtaining additional verification of the amounts involved;
- checking that the format and basis of preparation of the accounts accords with the requirements of the Regulations.

In addition, where accounts are prepared on the accruals basis, the independent examiner must check them for compliance with the Regulations in terms of format and content, review accounting policies, estimates and judgements, enquire about post-balance sheet events and compare the accounts with the trustees' report to make sure they are consistent with each other.

The independent examiner should inform the Charity Commission, in writing, if he or she has reasonable cause to believe that one or more of the trustees has been responsible for deliberate or reckless misconduct in the administration of the charity.

Who can be an independent examiner?

The Charities Act 1993 defines an independent examiner as 'an independent person who is reasonably believed by the trustees to have the requisite ability and practical experience to carry out a competent examination of the accounts'. It went on to define independent as having 'no connection with the charity's trustees which might inhibit the impartial conduct of the examination'. Therefore the independent examiner should be competent and familiar with accountancy methods but need not be a practising accountant. Someone with a professional qualification, preferably a qualified accountant, is strongly recommended by the Charity Commission. This is particularly so for the larger charities or where accruals accounting is adopted.

The independent examiner's report

The content of the report is determined by the Regulations. It must state:
- the name and address of the examiner and the name of the charity;
- the date of the report and the financial year to which the relevant accounts relate;
- reference to the report being carried out under Section 43 of the Charities Act 1993;
- whether or not matters have come to the independent examiner's attention which give him/her reasonable cause to believe that:
  - proper accounting records have not been maintained;
  - the accounts do not agree with the accounting records;
  - where accruals accounts are prepared, that the Regulations for form and content of the accounts have not been complied with;

- whether or not any matter has come to his/her attention which should be referred to in the accounts;
- by exception, if there have been any of the following:
  - material expenditure or action contrary to the trusts of the charity;
  - withholding of information or explanations due to him/her;
  - where accruals accounts are prepared, inconsistencies between the accounts and the trustees' report.

The report must be signed by the independent examiner and must state any relevant professional qualifications or professional body of which he or she is a member. The recommended reporting requirements are set higher than the compliance reports for companies under the deregulation regime.

In summary

The *Directions and Guidance Notes* (CC63), a revised version of CC56, published by the Charity Commission on 'Independent Examination of Accounts under SORP 2000' should be read by all charities that are going to be independently examined and must be read by those carrying out such examinations.

Whistle-blowing

This 'whistle-blowing' duty, as set in the Regulations, is a provision designed to increase public confidence by giving the auditor or independent examiner of an unincorporated charity the right and duty to report certain facts direct to the Charity Commission. This will occur if acting in their capacity of auditor or independent examiner they find evidence of deliberate or reckless misconduct by one or more trustees, especially action (or often more appropriately inaction) which puts the property of the charity at risk. Matters that are of material significance have to be reported to the Charity Commission.

Auditors are not required to change the scope of their work to discover whether or not reportable matters exist. The duty arises if something is discovered whilst carrying out their audit which in their opinion is judged to be of 'material significance'. The APB Practice Note, in dealing with this duty at paragraphs 4–31 and commenting on SAS

620, sets out in some detail the three main types of material significant matters likely to be reportable:

- a significant inadequacy of the arrangements made by the trustees for the direction and management of a charity's affairs;
- a significant breach of a legislative requirement or of the charity's trusts; or
- circumstances indicating a probably deliberate misuse of charity property.

It is expected that the revised APB Practice Note will be extended further in its advice on the requirements to 'whistle blow'.

Directory

Further reading

Charity Accounts and Reports: Core Guide (Stationery Office, 1996). Includes a copy of the Regulations, relevant extracts from the legislation and a commentary.

Dawes, Greyham, *Tolley's Charity Accountability and Compliance* (Tolley Publishing Co. Ltd, 1999). A comprehensive guide explaining the different ways in which charities must account for their funds.

Derwent, Richard & Richardson, Jane, *Charities: An Industry Accounting and Auditing Guide* (Accountancy Books, 1997). Guide that covers all significant aspects of accounting, auditing and taxation as it relates to charities.

Gambling, Trevor & Jones, Rowan, *The Financial Governance of Charities* (Charities Aid Foundation, 1996). Focuses on the financial administration of voluntary organisations, in terms of budgetary planning, expenditure patterns and accounting procedures. Also examines the role of trustees.

Gillingham, Shirley & Tame, John, *Not Just for a Rainy Day?* (NCVO Publications, 1997). Guidelines on developing a reserves policy and putting it into practice. Includes case studies and sample policy statements.

Grant, Ian Caulfield, *The Treasurer's Handbook* (Charities Aid Foundation, 1996). This book outlines a treasurer's key tasks, and explains the basics of financial management for those involved in the voluntary sector.

Haroon, Bashir, *The Good Financial Management Guide* (NCVO Publications, 1997). Guide aimed at helping organisations to run their finances efficiently and effectively.

Manley, Keith, *Financial Management for Charities and Voluntary Organisations* (ICSA Publishing Ltd, 1994). A practical introduction to financial management containing real examples and case studies.

Moss, Gail, *Money Management: Banking* (Charities Aid Foundation, 1999). Step-by-step guide to banking for the small voluntary organisation.

Moss, Gail, *Money Management: Raising a Loan* (Charities Aid Foundation, 1999). Step-by-step guide to raising a loan for the small voluntary organisation.

Pharoah, Cathy, *A Delicate Balance: Survey of Financial Management in the Voluntary Sector* (Charities Aid Foundation, 1998). Reports on a survey assessing the state of financial management in the voluntary sector.

Pianca, Andrew, *Charity Accounts: A Practical Guide to the Charities SORP* (Jordan Publishing Ltd, 1998). Explains how accounts should be prepared and presented and provides examples of how different types of charity could tackle any problems that may occur.

Randall, Adrian, Epton, Anthony & Young, Fiona, *Preparing Charity Accounts* (Accountancy Books, 1999). A practical guide covering all the main topics necessary for producing good charity accounts.

Sargeant, Adrian & Kaehler, Juergen, *Benchmarking Charity Costs* (Charities Aid Foundation, 1998). Provides a range of statistics against which charity costs can be benchmarked. Examines the relationships between costs and the size of charity, fundraising and sources of income.

Sayer, Kate, *A Practical Guide to Financial Management for Charities* (Directory of Social Change, 1998). Detailed guide with examples covering the various aspects of financial management.

Sayer, Kate, *A Practical Guide to Accounting by Charities* (Directory of Social Change, 1996). Accounting and reporting requirements as required by SORP, with examples.

Vincent, Robert & Francis, Amanda, *Charity Accounting & Taxation* (Butterworth & Co. Ltd, 1994 (4th ed)). Comprehensive guide to the tax and accounting concerns of a charity, examining in-depth, statutory and other accounting requirements.

Whitehill, Clark, *Tolley's Client and Adviser Guide: Charities* (Tolley Publishing Co. Ltd, 1999). A practical guide to advising charities on the auditing and preparation of their accounts. Includes information on problem areas such as using 'value for money' techniques and choosing appropriate IT.

Wise, David, *Accounting and Finance for Charities: For Love and Money* (ICSA Publishing Ltd, 1998). Comprehensive guide to the key financial issues facing charities includes self-assessment exercises so that readers can test their understanding of the guide.

Other sources of information

Charity Commission leaflets

The following are some of the leaflets that are produced by the Charity Commission. They can be obtained free of charge from – Charity Commission, Distribution Office, Woodfield House, Tangier, Taunton, Somerset TA1 4BL. Tel: 0870 333 0123 or 01823 345427. They can also be printed directly from their WWW site at: <http.//www.charity-commission.gov.uk>
Internal Financial Controls for Charities (CC8)
Investment of Charitable Funds: Basic Principles (CC14)
Charity Accounts 2001: The Framework (CC61)
Charities SORP 2000: What Has Changed (CC62)
Independent Examination of Accounts under SORP 2000: Direction and guidance notes (CC63)
SORP 2000: Receipts and Payments Accounts Pack (CC64)
SORP 2000: Accruals Accounts Pack (CC65)
SORP 2000: Example Reports and Accounts (CC66) – Accounting and reporting by charities: Statement of Recommended Practice.

Journals

Corporate Citizen
Focuses on how corporate support works and on how to raise funds from companies. For subscription information contact: Directory of Social Change, 24 Stephenson Way, London NW1 2DP. Tel: 020 7209 0902; Fax: 020 7209 4130.

Charity Finance
  Information for non-governmental organisations, and charities which focuses on investment, tax, law and other financial matters. For subscription information contact. Charity Finance, 3 Rectory Grove, London SW4 0DX. Tel: 020 7819 1200; Fax: 020 7819 1210; E-mail: team@charityfinance.co.uk

Accountancy
  Focuses on the general issues surrounding the world of accounting, including changes in law etc. For subscription information contact: institute of Chartered Accountants, 40 Bernard Street, London WC1N 1LD. Tel: 020 7833 3291; Fax: 020 7833 2085.

Management Accounting
  Provides information useful to accounting managers. For subscription information contact: Chartered Institute of Management Accountants, 63 Portland Place, London W1N 4AB. Tel: 020 7637 2311; Fax: 020 7631 5309.

Financial Accountability & Management in Government, Public Services and Charities
  International journal reporting areas of research in finance and management areas, for government and other non-profit organisations. For subscription information contact: Journals Customer Services, Blackwell Publishers Journals, PO Box 805, 108 Cowley Road, Oxford OX4 1FH. Tel: 01865 244083; Fax: 01865 381381; E-mail: jnlinfo@blackwellpublishers.co.uk

Financial Reporting for Charities Package
  Provides advice on financial planning, taxation, as well as guidance on producing financial statements. New and replacement pages are issued to subscribers every six months. For subscription information contact: Croner House, London Road, Kingston upon Thames, Surrey KT2 6SR. Tel: 020 8547 3333; Fax 020 8547 2637; E-mail: info@croner.co.uk

Financial advisors

There are many financial advisors that specialise in charity work. There is a list of charity financial advisors with contact details in:

Charity Logistics Charity Buyers Guide (Perspective Publishing Ltd, 1998).

UK Top 10,000 Charities on CD ROM (CaritasData, 2001). Charities Direct have also compiled a list of 'Auditors and their Charity Clients' and 'Financial Advisors and their Charity Clients' which can be found at: <http://www.caritasdata.co.uk>

Useful addresses

Charities Aid Foundation (CAF)
Kings Hill
West Malling
Kent
ME19 4TA
Tel: 01732 520000
Fax: 01732 520001
E-mail: enquiries@caf.charitynet.org
Provides services to charities to assist in the management of their funds.

Charity Finance Directors Group (CFDG)
Camelford House
87–89 Albert Embankment
London SE1 7TP
Tel: 020 7793 1400
Fax: 020 7793 1600
E-mail: info@cfdg.org.uk
Provides training and information on financial management.

Charities Advisory Trust
Radius Works, Back Lane
Hampstead
London NW3 1HL
Tel: 020 7794 9835
Fax: 020 7431 3739
E-mail: charities.advisory.trust@ukonline.co.uk
Provides advice on all aspects of charity trading.

Association of Charitable Foundations
2 Plough Yard
Shoreditch High Street
London EC2A 3LP
Tel: 020 7422 8600
Fax: 020 7422 8606
E-mail: acf@acf.org.uk
Helps trusts to use their funds effectively.

The Charity Service Limited
Gaddum House
6, Great Jackson Street
Manchester M15 4AX
Tel: 0161 839 3291
Fax: 0161 839 3298
E-mail: charity.service@dial.pipex.com
Assists charities by providing advice on raising funds through donors.

Useful WWW sites

Charities Aid Foundation (CAF)
    General information on CAF and the services it provides and links to other useful
    organisations
    <http://www.charitynet.org/caf/nav.html>
Association of Charitable Foundations
    General information on the Association and the services it provides including
    details of its publications.
    <http://www.acf.org.uk>
Charities Advisory Trust
    Information on the research, publications and training provided by the Charities
    Advisory Trust.
    <http://web.ukonline.co.uk/charities.advisory.trust/>

Index

expenditure, 49–52
format, 36–7
fund accounting, 20, 36
gains/losses, 52–3
incoming resources, 41–8
operating activities, 44–7
structure, 37–9
Statement of Recommended Practice
    (SORP), 5–8, 11, 14–22
Statements of Standard Accounting
    Practice (SSAP), 16
SSAP 4, 41
SSAP 10, 66
Statements of Auditing Standards (SAS),
    134–5, 141–2
statistics, 122–3
statutory reports, audits, 141–2
subsidiaries, 100–7
    checklist, 107
    definition, 101–2
    exclusions, 100
summary financial information, 91–9
    audits/examinations, 92–3
    content, 91–2
    examples, 94–9
    full accounts, 94
    incorporated charities, 93, 118
summary income and expenditure
    accounts, 114–17
support costs, 51

thresholds, 9–10
    audits, 10, 130
    cash flow statements, 67
    functional classifications, 48
    grants, 17
    independent examinations, 10, 143
    smaller charities, 9, 16, 119, 143
    trustees' report, 24
true and fair view, 71, 100, 133
trustees' expenses, 76–7, 82
trustees' reports, 16, 23–33
    Charities Act (1993), 23
    example, 29–33
    Regulations, 24
    requirements, 26
    smaller charities, 24, 121, 124
    SORP, 24–6
    stakeholders 26–29
trustees' roles, 2, 16, 23–5, 91–3
Turnbull Report, 25

undertakings, definition, 102
unrestricted funds, 19–21, 53

valuations, 55–6, 62–3
voluntary donations see donations
voluntary help, 43

'whistle-blowing', 145–6
Wise, David, 29